DON JOHNSON
An Unauthorized Biography

THE FLESH AND BLOOD BENEATH THE PASTEL T-SHIRT

On the TV screen, he's an image of sexy good looks and even sexier world-weariness as he and his partner go after the bad guys in a world of Miami vice he clearly knows very well.

Those close to him in real life know a different Don Johnson.

Patti D'Arbanville, his lover and mother of his two-and-a-half-year-old son, knows him as a man who desperately needed her help in kicking the habits that almost destroyed him.

His co-star on *Miami Vice*, Philip Michael Thomas, knows the truth about the rumors of Don Johnson's out-of-control ego and arrogance.

The people in his past, from the high school teacher who put him on the acting path to the women who were close to him during his years of obsessive sex, knew him at his best and at his worst.

Now for the first time you, too, will know the *real* Don Johnson, so gifted and so all-too-very human.

About the Author

Suzanne Munshower, author of bestselling biographies of John Travolta, Diane Keaton and Warren Beatty, is one of America's top celebrity chroniclers.

Don Johnson

An unauthorized
biography

Suzanne
Munshower

Produced by Ultra
Communications Inc.

NEW ENGLISH LIBRARY
Hodder and Stoughton

Copyright © 1986 by Ultra Communications

First published in the United States
in 1986 by New American Library

New English Library Paperback Edition 1987

British Library C.I.P.

Don Johnson: an unauthorized biography.
1. Johnson, Don 2. Television actors and actresses—
United States—Biography 3. Miami vice (Television
program)
I. Title
791.45′028′0924   PN2287.J5/

ISBN 0-450-41119-2

Printed and bound in Great Britain for
Hodder and Stoughton Paperbacks, a
division of Hodder and Stoughton Ltd.,
Mill Road, Dunton Green, Sevenoaks,
Kent (Editorial Office: 47 Bedford
Square, London WC1B 3DP) by
Richard Clay Ltd., Bungay, Suffolk

ACKNOWLEDGMENTS

The author would like to thank the
following for their help in researching
this biography:

Dee Anne Johnson, from Wichita,
and all her friends at Wichita South;
KSN-TV, Wichita; Geraldine Duclow, the
Theatre Collection, and Maggie Hassett,
the Data Research Department, of the
Free Library of Philadephia; in L.A.,
Ann Bogart and Dianna Whitley; in N.Y.,
Sonja Wagner and Karen Williams.

Contents

Prologue

Every fall, television sets across America become the repositories of hopes, dreams, and disappointments. Each new season, according to ABC, NBC, and CBS, the three major American television networks, is going to be the best yet. Viewers, bored and weary after the summer's reruns, are assaulted by a barrage of adjectives raining upon them like so much "friendly fire." Having grown wary after so many years of hype, most viewers know enough to duck. How often have those "original," "exciting," "inventive," "thrilling" new series turned out to be *Gilligan's Island,* *My Mother the Car,* or just another rip-off of last year's biggest success?

The prerelease accolades being churned out by the NBC publicity department had the familiar flavor of hype back in the summer of '84. Could this *Miami Vice* live up to the promise of being as revolutionary as the network insisted it would be? Seasoned television viewers and critics greeted the fanfare with suspicion. *Miami Vice* promised to be just another cop show, *The Rookies Gone South, Starsky and Hutch at the Orange Bowl.*

It didn't matter that this series was supposed to take up where MTV left off. Since when did rock-and-roll belong on a police show, anyhow? If NBC was so clever, wouldn't they have come up with something closer to the smash *Hill Street Blues,* something gritty and unglamorous? And wouldn't they have signed some real stars instead of an unknown named Philip Michael Thomas and a has-been like Don Johnson? Expectations were high only within NBC itself, as the rest of America anticipated the debut of what sounded like no more than a throwback to the slick studio-system series of the sixties, maybe a *77 Sunset Strip* or *Surfside Six* with a little New Wave music thrown in to fool viewers into believing that what they were seeing was very "now" instead of a great big dose of "then."

A lot of people had, to use one of Don Johnson's favorite words, a "major" surprise in store. On September 16, 1984, *Miami Vice* made a two-hour debut, and all of a sudden, the summer's hype became the fall's understatement. *Miami Vice* was everything NBC-TV had promised—and much more. It was like nothing else on TV that season, or any other season. It was new, and that was news.

Reviewing the opening show in the *Los Angeles Herald Examiner,* style editor David Gritten exulted that "this show makes most of the other current prime-time fare look as interesting as dead cold fish on a slab."

Strong words, but no stronger than the words other critics were bandying about. Richard Jameson warned, "Sit down to watch an episode of *Miami Vice* and you run the risk of being caught talking to yourself: It's hard to forbear saying, every five minutes or so, I can't believe this was shot for *television!*"

John Leonard devoted two entire articles in *New York* to philosophizing about the remarkable new series. Sally Bedell Smith, writing in the *New York Times*, called the show "aggressively contemporary." And Rick Du Brow said *Miami Vice* was "so bursting with energy that at times it seems to strain to explode out of the restrictive borders of the 19-inch living-room TV screen."

3

Almost overnight *Miami Vice* turned out to be the most critically acclaimed show of the 1984 television season. Just as quickly, Don Johnson went from being yet another has-been to wearing the label "the sexiest man on TV."

No one was more dazzled by it all than Don Johnson himself. Hollywood's hottest new star—who'd gone from Flatt Creek, Missouri, to Wichita, Kansas, to the starring role in a major film when he was barely out of his teens, and then had kept on going through drugs and alcohol—had been ready to throw in the towel shortly before the role of Sonny Crockett on *Miami Vice* came his way.

Now, with success safely his, the overnight discovery of the eighties could survey his future with buoyant satisfaction and proclaim, "I've come a long way from the heartland." Most of his journey has been too precipitously downhill for Don Johnson ever to take his newfound fame and fortune lightly. He has earned his success the hard way, making his stardom even more brilliant.

1

MTV Cops

Brandon Tartikoff is one of the Hollywood whiz kids, the new generation of "baby moguls" who eat, sleep, and breathe TV and movies. Just thirty when he was named NBC president of entertainment, Tartikoff is given a royal share of the credit when network chairman Grant Tinker talks about NBC's phenomenal success.

Critics are calling NBC "the Cinderella network" because of its rapid rise from the network no one took seriously to, in the summer of 1985, the network with fourteen consecutive weeks in the number-one spot.

When Tinker was brought in to replace Fred

Silverman in July of 1981, he brought with him a philosophy that would go a long way toward turning young Brandon Tartikoff into the network's Prince Charming. Tinker believed the only way to revitalize the network was to "try to attract to NBC the best creative people, make them comfortable, give them whatever help they need, and then get the hell out of the way."

It was a philosophy with which Brandon Tartikoff could live and under which he would thrive. Tartikoff, the son of a Long Island clothing manufacturer, was an idea man, had been an idea man since his days as an English major at Yale.

It was at Yale that Brandon studied with novelist (*All the King's Men*) Robert Penn Warren. One day, during a tutorial, Tartikoff was called upon to analyze a story by D. H. Lawrence. Instead of critiquing the material as written, Brandon asked, "Wouldn't it be better if the girl had first seen the guy over here in his other setting, and then met the other person over there?" Warren stared for a moment, then suggested Tartikoff consider going into television.

That's exactly what Brandon, with a B.A. in English under his belt, decided to do, starting out at a New Haven television station while he pursued his other great love, baseball, by playing semipro for the New Haven Braves.

His route to NBC was a short one, with one stop-off at WLS-TV in Chicago. At the network offices, it wasn't long before word got around that Tartikoff was prone to scribbling memos, and that his memos had more meat in them than many fifty-page series proposals.

Producer Steven Cannell came up with *The A-Team* after receiving a memo from Tartikoff which read, "*Road Warrior, Magnificent Seven, Dirty Dozen, Mission: Impossible,* all rolled into one, and Mr. T drives the car."

The Cosby Show was born after Brandon phoned Bill's agent and suggested, "A black *Family Ties.*"

But perhaps the most important memo Tartikoff ever jotted was the one that said simply, "MTV cops."

The memo went to Anthony Yerkovich, a thirty-four-year-old former writer and producer for *Hill Street Blues,* where it struck a chord. Yerkovich had a movie idea, about a pair of vice cops in Miami, and he saw no reason why it couldn't fuse with Tartikoff's vague concept and become a television series.

"Even when I was on *Hill Street Blues,* I was collecting information on Miami," Yerkovich would later tell *Time* magazine. "I thought of it as a sort of modern-day American *Casablanca*. It seemed to be an interesting socioeconomic tidepool: the incredible number of refugees from Central America and Cuba, the already extensive Cuban-American community, and on top of all that the drug trade. There is a fascinating amount of service industries that revolve around the drug trade—money laundering, bail bondsmen, attorneys who service drug smugglers. Miami has become a sort of Barbary Coast of free enterprise gone berserk."

Yerkovich called the pilot script about the city described by *TV Guide* as "*Casablanca* with cocaine and cabanas" *Gold Coast*. Shortly before the series debuted, the name was changed to *Miami Vice*.

Emmy-winner Yerkovich had no trouble relating to Tartikoff's concept of "MTV cops." He liked the idea of using MTV-style visuals as well as contemporary music. He agreed with Tartikoff, and with everyone who would come to be connected with the show, that television had long needed something new.

"It's not just TV's subject matter that lags, but its visual reflexes," he said. "Younger audiences have a much quicker grasp of visual information now. Network TV has such a stodgy narrative pace that it's almost impossible to stay involved with a show unless you're doing something a little more interesting in the background—like building a nuclear warhead."

Enter Michael Mann, forty-one, another of the entertainment business's young, hip breed. These men weren't Yuppies. They didn't wear three-piece suits and Bass Weejuns. They leaned toward Hawaiian shirts and New Balance running shoes. And they knew that other Americans in their age group were doing the same thing they were doing—watching MTV not so much for the rock-and-roll but for the visuals, the flashy editing, the indescribable *feeling* communicated by the sum of a video's parts.

Executive producer Mann wears sweat pants to the office, lights one cigarette after another, and drinks black coffee as if it were Gatorade. His instincts about what would become *Miami Vice* more than mirrored Yerkovich's. Mann more keenly wanted to make the series something that had never before hit the television screens.

As far as Mann was concerned, the time for a radically different police series had arrived. "Television *has* to do this," he affirmed. "I mean, you can't have this stuff from 1974 on the air in 1984 and flip over the channel and pick up *Scarface* and expect to compete."

To the role of executive producer, Mann

brought a director's eye, along with an Emmy he'd won for directing *The Jericho Mile*. He also brought a background in establishing a mood through carefully choreographed visuals, something he'd achieved as director of the James Caan starrer, *Thief,* and the visually striking box-office failure, *The Keep.*

"My real point is that network TV is very reactionary these days," he told the *Los Angeles Times* in the fall of 1984. "I can't even watch two minutes of a show like *The Dukes of Hazzard;* it's so crude and simplistic that it's completely antiquated in any real cultural sense—it's yesterday's newspapers. Just look at some of the shows on the air today. All the women are walking around as if they were still in the '60s, both in the way they talk as well as the way they look.

"If network TV doesn't move into the '80s and become more relevant, they're going to find all their viewers switching to cable before they know what hit them."

Mann's plan for moving into the eighties had three prongs: visuals, music, and attitude.

The visuals would be vivid, strikingly lit, and shot from any angle that looked interesting, then edited to keep the pace frenetic. Mann was determined to break rules, to "cut wherever I feel like it" in order to get the look he wanted.

10

The music would feature hits by popular rock singers and groups, intercut so they underscored the action.

The attitude would be hip, non-Hollywood, using character actors who would bring as much individuality to guest roles and supporting spots as the stars. Dialogue would be current street talk and drug patter. Dress would be chic and funky, spotlighting the type of high-priced togs worn by Cher or Steven Bishop and not Mary Tyler Moore or Larry Hagman.

"Style," Mann intoned. "It's the key to this whole show if we're going to get the feel of the milieu right. If we need to shoot a scene in a sleazy location, I want us to use a sleazy Art Deco location, not just some distressed neighborhood dump. You know, not every show on TV has to look like it was shot on the Universal back lot."

No detail was overlooked as Mann, along with producer John Nicolella, considered every color used by the wardrobe and art departments. The directive was, tertiary colors only. That meant no earth tones, no reds. *Ever.* Instead, art director Jeffrey Howard came up with a whole tertiary palette of acid yellow, cobalt blue, gleaming black, violets, pastels. "I want a mint-green jacket against a peach-colored wall," Mann told Howard.

The look, the style were not going to come cheap. Making what Mann referred to as "little movies" meant the network backing a television series that was going to come in with a budget averaging about $1.3 million a week; it meant spending more than $10,000 per episode to buy the rights to original recordings instead of having made-for-TV imitations. It meant painstaking attention to the smallest detail.

Bobby Roth directed an episode of *Miami Vice* before moving over to ABC as executive producer of one of TV's *Miami Vice* copycat shows, *The Insiders*. He told a *Time* reporter, "There is a very definite attempt to give the show a particular look. There are certain colors you are not allowed to shoot, such as red and brown. If the script says 'A Mercedes pulls up here,' the car people will show you three or four different Mercedes. One will be white, one will be black, one will be silver. You will not get a red one or a brown one. Michael knows how things are going to look on camera. A lot of it is very basic stuff that has never been applied to TV. For example, Michael carried a water truck around with him on his movie *Thief,* watering the streets down. So I decided to water the streets at night in my episode of *Miami Vice.* You get a different look, a beautiful reflection of moonlight off the pavement."

For the same episode, Roth came up with a house that was perfect for an exterior shot. There was only one little hitch—the house was beige, an earth tone. That posed no problem for the *Miami Vice* art department, who promptly painted the house gray just for the shot. Roth was amazed and delighted, because "people try to deliver what is necessary but no more. At *Miami Vice,* they start with what's necessary and go beyond it."

With the series concept firmly decided upon and scripts in the works, the producers had only one thing left to do. A small thing it wasn't. They had to cast the program. They weren't especially worried about filling the secondary parts; there were more than a few talented character actors in Hollywood and New York who'd jump at the chance to play some roles they could really sink their teeth into. No, it was the job of casting the leads that presented the challenge.

A television series needs strong actors playing the leads, actors whose talent and charisma can carry the show on a weekly basis, actors whom the TV audience will tune in to watch even if the story line of that week's episode doesn't appeal to them, even if the guest stars aren't people they'd go out of their way to watch. When the advance word got out on *Miami Vice*—that it was going to be hot—the phone lines were burning up as actors called their agents and told them to do whatever was necessary to get them in for a reading or an interview.

One actor who'd heard about the upcoming series and wanted to be considered for it was Don Johnson. The only trouble was, he was about the last actor with whom any network wanted to associate itself. He was considered bad news.

Johnson had two major strikes against him. For one thing, his carousing from the time he had hit Hollywood back in 1970 was common knowledge. For another, he'd had a long string of failures, and it didn't seem possible that any series "starring Don Johnson" was going to be around for more than a single season at best.

It was Brandon Tartikoff who wanted at least to take a look at him, and there's no doubt that if the man wasn't the president of entertainment for the network, Johnson wouldn't have been considered as a contender. Perhaps he wouldn't even have been given the chance to read for the part.

But Tartikoff had clout, and he was quick to point out to his associates that Don Johnson wasn't the only good actor whose name was connected with one bad pilot after another. There was another guy who'd had a hard time getting a series because he always made one lousy pilot after another, pilots so unmemorable that few television viewers even knew who he was when he'd finally gotten that one last chance to make it. That actor was Tom Selleck, and *Magnum, P.I.* has more than made up for every dog of a show he'd done in the past.

But everyone else made it clear to Tartikoff that they didn't share his optimism about Don Johnson. "I really didn't want him in it," Michele Brustin, NBC vice-president, later admitted. "There was a negative feeling left over from his past. He'd done a pilot for us, *Six Pack,* two years before. He looked too soft, didn't have that edge."

Johnson knew the score. He'd been around, and he knew his stock in the TV marketplace was at its worst. He went after the part, fighting yet unwilling to get carried away with hoping, for four long months, even bending a personal rule and doing a screen test in the hopes that something, *anything,* would convince the network he was cut out to be Sonny Crockett.

Even with Tartikoff as a booster, Don was considered a dark horse. NBC kept him on a back burner as they saw actor after actor,

15

and all Johnson could do was concentrate on the task at hand, starring in a low-budget film, *Cease Fire,* in Florida, and try not to build up his hopes.

The year before he'd come close to packing it all in, moving back to Missouri, where he'd been born, and trying his hand at farming. That's how low things had sunk. Now he could only wait and wonder. Would he meet defeat and return with busted hopes and broken dreams to the heartland he'd worked so hard to escape?

2

The Heartland

Don Johnson was born in Missouri, the "Show Me State," whose population is less than twice that of Los Angeles. Most of his formative years were spent in Kansas, the population of which is less than L.A.'s. He has come a long way from the heartland.

Don was born in his grandmother's cabin, located—depending on which story you hear—in Galena or Flatt Creek, Missouri. Like so many of the flatland states, Missouri is largely agricultural. Soybeans and corn are grown there, as are winter wheat, cotton, and hay. Missouri has its industrial side, too, especially in transport: autos and aircraft are manufactured there. Beer is brewed, flour is milled, meat is packed. Only 10 percent of the population is black, and the countryside abounds in deer, wild turkey, and bears. It's a far cry from Miami, the city that brought Don Johnson fame, a polyglot melting pot where tourism and drug-dealing are two of the big moneymakers for private investors.

Don was Wayne and Nell Johnson's firstborn. Don describes his father as a jack-of-all-trades, and it's true the elder Johnson has had a variety of careers. He's a master mechanic and a carpenter who has ranched and worked as a contractor. When Don was born, Wayne Johnson was working his mother's farm.

The family's background was religious rather than theatrical—Don's aunt, Clymena Bell, was an evangelist, and both his grandfathers were preachers. Don's first taste of the limelight came when he was just four or five, singing solos in church.

"I'd sing 'Rock of Ages,' and people would pinch my cheek," he said of those early years, "say, 'Aren't you wonderful?' and give me a quarter. I'm sure I was bitten by the bug then, because of the affection and the money."

Don was just about five when the Johnsons moved to Wichita, where Wayne started working for an aircraft company and Nell decided to be a beautician. Soon, there were other children. Today Don's sister Linda, who uses the name Jamie Skylar, is a singer/songwriter; the next oldest child, Greg, works as a glass cutter in Missouri; while brother K.C. manages an auto-parts department in California.

Nell and Wayne divorced when Don was just eleven. The divorce's effect on the boy, as he told a reporter from *Rolling Stone* many years later, was, "Devastating. More than I was willing to admit. But at the time I was pleased, because there'd been a lot of fighting in the house. My parents just weren't in love anymore. They got married when my father was eighteen and my mother fifteen. I was born when she was sixteen. Nevertheless, the divorce was a shocker, because right there, in one instant, life changed. Suddenly there were major choices I had to make that you shouldn't have to make when you're eleven years old. I realized then it was dog eat dog, every man for himself. However, even before they were divorced, I never really felt a part of the family, even though I'm very caring, loving, careful, and considerate of them. I knew I was going to go off and do other things."

It wasn't an especially easy childhood,

though he's claimed it was neither happy nor unhappy, rather "a nice artistic blend of both."

Others don't remember it being such a blend. Bobby Stout, former deputy police chief of Wichita and a family friend, remembers Don having to take care of his brothers and sister while his mother worked long hours to take care of the family. Stout also recalls that Don wasn't fond of the men Nell later married and also divorced, and Don himself has admitted that he deeply resented his father's new wife when his dad rewed not long after the divorce.

When he was shooting *The Magic Garden of Stanley Sweetheart,* Don compared himself to the title character, a youth who was rather lost and who got into one scrape after another in his search for identity. "It's a fortuitous coincidence," Don said then (little knowing what a bomb the movie would turn out to be), "but in many respects my bag is also Stanley's. I've experienced the same trips, the same struggles to find myself. So many people my age have had to take the measure of responsibility and reality that I think they will really appreciate Stanley and what he represents. . . . I was on my own, and I had to do most anything to make bread. I was like Stanley in my confusion. I knew there was something better and I was searching but I didn't know what exactly it was that I wanted. Finally I settled into my magic garden—acting."

Even before he started acting, he was charming the opposite sex. "Was I fat and ugly as a kid? No," Don said in 1985. "The girls used to carry me around and kiss me in the halls at school. I was pretty."

According to Don, he was also sexually active at an early age, losing his virginity at the age of twelve to a seventeen-year-old baby-sitter. His jocular remark on the subject: "I was supposedly old enough to take care of myself, and apparently, my mother was right about that."

Being the oldest sibling in a broken home doesn't bring many rewards, though, and as Uthona Tole, one of the Johnsons' neighbors, remembers, "Responsibility was kind of thrust on him rather early in life." Describing Don as "a kid who might have gone either way," Tole, who still lives in the old neighborhood in Wichita, recalls that Don "had a pretty good head on his shoulders, and his mother instilled in him enough common sense to stay out of trouble."

Nowadays, Don seems to be trying to put Wichita behind him, though he spent most of his formative years there. He usually tells reporters he was born in Missouri and leaves it at that, and according to his former high-school buddies, he hasn't set foot in the Kansas town since his mother's funeral in 1975.

But then, it's sometimes difficult to separate fact from fantasy in Johnson's own reminiscences; for instance, though he never changes the date of his birth (December 15, 1949), he sometimes says his grandmother's house was in Flatt Creek, sometimes Galena. He always gives his high-school drama teacher, Karen (Pyles) Slater credit for getting him interested in acting—and there's no doubt she was a major influence in his adolescence—but he doesn't bother mentioning that he had already appeared on stage in 1963, when he was at Truesdell Junior High in Wichita.

Johnson also seems to prefer his picture of himself as a "hell raiser" rather than a genuinely troubled child who couldn't adjust to his parents' divorce or new mates.

Whether he was just "mischievous" (as he puts it) or miserable, the truth is he got into trouble when he was just twelve. He and a buddy hot-wired a car and went joy riding. Though the friend was driving, it was Don who'd hot-wired the motor, so the friend got off while Don was sent to juvenile hall, convicted of "grand theft auto." He was remanded to the detention home for just a couple of weeks, but that was long enough, he admitted, "to make me realize that it wasn't the place for me."

Upon leaving the facility, he was sent to live with his father and his father's new wife. Wayne Johnson was still living in Kansas then, but he soon decided to return to Missouri, where he opened up a small country store and garage. Don recently told Nancy Collins that it was "when we left Wichita [that] my problems at home really began. It was my age, my stepmother, whom I resented, and the fact that I had a reputation for being a bad guy. . . ."

When Don was sixteen, he ran away, back to Wichita, knowing he'd have to graduate from high school if he was ever going to make it on his own in the world. But he wasn't going back to live with Nell and his brothers and sister. Instead he lived with friends of the family—until he moved in with a twenty-six-year-old cocktail waitress.

Lost though he may have been, Don found out something about himself after starting his senior year at Wichita South High School that was to change his whole life and lead him, eventually, down a long and winding road to *Miami Vice*.

"I was fairly lost," Don has said of the

beginning of his senior year in high school. "I didn't really know what I wanted to do. I thought I wanted to play professional ball or be an athlete of some sort, but I wasn't really tall enough, fast enough, or good enough."

Now, of course, he gets to play an ex-football star every week. Then he was a wide receiver on Wichita South's team. "Then one day I was sitting in a business class and I kept falling asleep, so the teacher threw me out. I went in to the counselor and she said that the only class left open was at the end of the day and would interfere with football practice. She said it was a drama class. I said, 'Are you kidding? Isn't that for guys who are a little, uh, light in their loafers?' " When the counselor pointed out that he'd need the credit if he wanted to graduate, Don decided acting might not be such a bad thing, after all.

He didn't realize until he tried it how well being on stage fit his personality. As his old friend Jim Oaks recalls, "He was a poor student who didn't enjoy classes. What he enjoyed doing was playing, and once he got into theater, he enjoyed that."

Getting in wasn't all that easy. Karen Pyles, now Karen Slater, asked Don, "Are you taking my class because you want a credit, or can you really do anything?" She told him he'd have to audition for the school play, *West Side Story,* before he'd be allowed in the class.

The guidance counselor responsible for his seeing Karen Slater was Lorene (Stone) Yabrof, who recently reminisced, "He came bouncing into my office saying, 'I have the lead in *West Side Story!*' From there he just took off. Don was friendly, outgoing, and had lots of personality. Maybe *he* didn't feel that way, but he was. He'd come into my office singing. He made your day."

According to Don, his love for acting was "Instant! It struck something in me that was true and real. It was like having lost one's mother and all of a sudden being reunited. And when she (Slater) saw that, she started handing me Tennessee Williams, Faulkner, and Albee to read. I was insatiable. For the first time in my life, I felt that I belonged to something."

Don has said that "a lot of people who helped smarten me up pointed out that an education went along with [a little bit of cash in your pocket]." Two of the people who went a long way in smartening him up were Lorene Yabrof and Karen Slater. "I'm sure they must have felt a great sense of accomplishment for saving a mixed-up, rather confused kid's life and giving him a future.

That's really the truth. I don't know what would have happened had I not run into those two ladies. I shudder to think what would have happened."

Drama offered Don a way out, an escape from not only his parents' marital difficulties but from "drinking beer, hanging out with my girlfriend, and raising hell with my buddies."

Acting was simply the best thing that had ever happened to him. "I finally found something I loved. And after three or four performances I knew this was for me. I even got good reviews!"

The 1967 *Sabre,* Wichita High School South's yearbook, has a two-page spread on *West Side Story,* titled "Romance, gang warfare paired in popular musical." Looking at the photos reproduced there, one can see— almost twenty years later—why Karen Pyles Slater thought Don had a future as an actor. There's a professionalism in his bearing the other student actors lack. As Don, playing Tony, stands over the body of rival gang leader Bernardo, realizing he's killed the other boy, the others in the photograph fade away into insignificant props. There's a tension, a studied posture in Don's body that rivets the viewer's attention. Obviously, he was a natural.

Getting involved with his high school's theater group and fine-arts department cemented Don's popularity and brought him friendships. Nick Mendoza, who played Bernardo, and Jimmy Oaks, who portrayed Chino in *West Side Story*, ended up being two of Don's best buddies through senior year.

Even though he was a late bloomer, Don earned the ten points needed for membership in National Thespian Society Troupe #182 and got to attend the formal banquet at the Civic Playhouse in May. But he'd plunged into theatrical activities too late to be a Troupe officer, even though his pal Jimmy Oaks was president.

Don also had a major role in the play that concluded the 1966–67 season, *Goodbye, My Fancy,* a drama on the "mature" side for a high-school production. The action revolved around the presentation of an honorary degree to a United States senator. Dramatic tension arose from the fact that the female senator had once dated a married professor at the college—and had been expelled for it, something the faculty had forgotten in deciding to award the honorary degree. Don had the meatiest role in the play, playing a photographer who was determined to expose the weak-willed professor and who was in love with the senator. While the school may

27

have been daring in its choice of subject matter, it was as old-fashioned as most high schools when it came to portraying the press. Don is shown wearing a porkpie hat and looking like a reporter from the thirties era of *The Front Page*.

Once bitten by the acting bug, young Don quickly changed his mind about actors being "light in their loafers." His commitment to the theater was immediate and total. "I loved the attention the theater gave you. I hated to leave sports, but I was bitten by the bug and I grew to love the theater. I liked the 'let's-put-on-a-show' attitude."

Slater and Johnson still talk about each other with mutual respect and admiration. She says, "Without him we probably couldn't have done *West Side Story*. He was extremely talented—a natural on stage—with a beautiful tenor voice."

Still teaching at Wichita South, Karen Slater remains loyal to her most famous student, explaining, "Don has such insight into human behavior, and he always underplayed his role. That was his strength. I use him as an example in my classes now. If I want my students to pick up a certain technique, I'll tell them to watch Don."

As for the famous student himself, he's said he "just ate it up" when his teacher gave him plays by artists like Shakespeare and Molière to read and discussed them with him. Describing himself as being "like a sponge" at the time, he says, "I started seeing life differently and became involved in cultural events around the city."

Through drama, his knowledge and popularity were growing. But his teen years weren't spent wholly on the stage. And his experiences in working part-time, hanging out with the guys, and wowing the girls went a long way toward shaping the Don Johnson his fans love on *Miami Vice*.

3

The Charisma Kid

In *Goodbye, My Fancy,* a pretty, dark-haired girl named Anna Davis played Agatha Reed, the senator beloved by photographer Matt Cole (Don Johnson). Off stage, Davis and Johnson were romantically involved as well, and their relationship seems to typify Johnson's involvements in those days. That is, Anna was much more involved than Don.

Anna Davis was also in *West Side Story,* where she first met Don, though she didn't play his leading lady in that one. Davis, now married and living in Oklahoma, told Clark Spencer of the *Wichita Eagle-Beacon,* "I remember the first day of school because Karen came running out and saying, 'I found Tony.' She pointed out Don to me and I went 'Yech!' I just didn't think he was that good-looking."

She soon changed her mind, and was so crazy about Don that, at one party where she got tired of his flirting with other girls, she literally ripped off his shirt! Unfortunately, the shirt didn't belong to Don—it was his stepfather's—but Johnson's ability to charm women of all ages saved the day when the mother of one of his friends took pity on him and went off to buy him an undamaged version of the exact same shirt.

Don and Anna's dates were mostly for plays and movies at the drive-in, and since Don couldn't afford a car, they either double-dated or borrowed the Davis family automobile. It was a high-pitched, emotional relationship, and according to Anna, when the times were good, "we were really in love, and when we were fighting, we were really fighting."

Anna Davis was one of Don's *many* high-school girlfriends; he didn't want to get tied down when he had such big dreams for the future. Kris Knuth was yet another of those with stars in their eyes over Don, and she beamed happily at his side during Wichita South's "Moonlight and Roses" junior-senior prom in January. It was a measure of Don's newfound popularity that, though he'd re-

31

turned to Wichita only that fall, he and Kris were senior attendants for the prom king and queen.

So intense was Don's effect on the opposite sex when he was just a teenager that the women who knew him then still gush over him twenty years later. Anna Davis Clark calls him "a charmer," while Lorene Yabrof says she's a fan. "I wasn't surprised at his success. Any role he played he put his whole person into. And many girls were swooning over him. He still has those beautiful, expressive eyes."

As for Karen Slater, she had the following comment when watching an episode of *Miami Vice:* "He's still the same old Don . . . he exudes self-confidence, breaking into that easy smile. But he looks older; that's good—the pretty face has developed some character lines. And he uses more facial expressions than he did. He's matured and grown in his acting ability; the changes are beneficial."

Nell Johnson, with four children to support, didn't have the easiest of times making ends meet, so Don had to balance acting and flirting with some old-fashioned working for a living. The actor who calls himself "an expert on b.s." seems to have used more than a little of that product himself back in Wichita when it came to getting a job. Today he likes to tell people that he once worked at a meat market conning customers into buying suspicious beef; he laughingly told one reporter, "I had one of those faces that people trusted, the poor suckers."

The owner of Kline's Meat Market remembers Don very well, but his memories didn't match up to those of his former employee. Kline remembers that Don applied for a job under the pretense that he was a butcher, but was soon shown up for the novice he in fact was. Kline, who says Don worked at his store for no longer than six months, let the boy earn his wage packet by doing trim work, waiting on customers at the counter, and scraping the meat block. Recalling that his young worker "came to work a couple of times plastered," Kline says that, even then, Don was telling people he'd be a movie star one day.

As he finished high school, Don found support for his visions of stardom. He was one of eight students from the entire Midwest chosen for the University of Kansas's summer repertory theater. He also won a scholarship to the theater department there.

At the university in Lawrence, Don was no longer the star he'd been back in high school. He was just one of 22,000 students, a little fish in a big pond who dreamed of wider horizons away from the heartland.

His buddy Jimmy Oaks, who roomed with Don at school, remembers him as rarely attending classes. As far as Don was concerned, he was beyond classes in acting. He was ready for the big time. "At that point," he said recently, referring to college age, "everybody thinks they're going to become a great actor and save Broadway single-handedly. Of course, the rude awakening comes quick. If Brando wasn't going to do it, nobody was."

Another reason his studies didn't entrance Don was that he'd graduated from girls his own age to women, older women. Karen Slater has said that Don was always "obsessed" with older women. Certainly, some of his best relationships—both romantic and platonic—were with women his senior. In 1985, Don told *Rolling Stone* he liked older women because girls his "own age were still very much consumed with Victorian attitudes and principles, even though it was 1967. Nice girls just didn't, but older nice girls did. And that's what I was interested in."

Sex may not have been the entire answer. Don may have been drawn to older women because of his mother. Nell Wilson had been little more than a kid herself when she'd married Don's father. In 1967, she was just in her midthirties, a woman everyone liked but one who didn't seem to be overly centered and mature. Nor did she have a great rapport with her son then, leading Bobby Stout to later insist, "Don's mother truly loved him and was extremely proud of him. Maybe she just didn't show it like he expected."

She also didn't like the fact that he wanted to be an actor; at one point she even prevailed upon Stout to try to dissuade her son from pursuing his chosen career. But Don's belief in his ability was unshakable.

Don's affinity for older women had some bearing on his decision to quit K.U. before he'd gotten through his second year, a decision that upset his mother greatly.

At eighteen, Don started living with Anita Sorrels, one of his college professors and the twenty-nine-year-old mother of three children. Anita, described by Don as "dark-complexioned and hot looking," one day revealed to him that Ed Hastings, then the resident director of San Francisco's prestigious American Conservatory Theater, ACT, was coming to Lawrence to direct Igor Stravinsky's *The Rakes Progress*. Don, always with an eye for the main chance, bugged

Hastings until he was granted an audition. The audition was so good Don ended up with a grant for ACT, and he and Anita decided to spend the summer in California studying with the company.

Before they actually left, Anita decided she didn't need an eighteen-year-old boy living with her—not when he was seeing other women and causing her grief.

Don was on his own, but not for long. With that ole Missouri charm, he talked three of his friends into driving to San Francisco, where they found an apartment they could afford with the little bit of money they'd scraped together. There, with the intensity the folks at *Miami Vice* would one day be getting used to, Don started spending almost every hour of every day studying. He took classes in mime, juggling, dancing, acting, and diction. And, in a break not unlike the one he'd gotten back in Wichita South when he'd won the lead in *West Side Story* soon after moving back to Kansas, Don got his first professional acting job just two weeks after arriving on the West Coast.

Your Own Thing, a "little fluffball," came to town from Broadway, coproduced by ACT. Don read for it and got a part and felt like he had it made. He was eighteen, an Actors'

Equity member, and was getting paid $150 a week, decent money for 1968. Just getting paid for his work made Don feel he was destined for success.

It was while he was in San Francisco that Don got married for the first time, to a dancer also planning to end up on Broadway. About two months later, they woke up to the mistake they'd made and got an annulment.

It was also in San Francisco that Don met Sal Mineo. Mineo, who'd been a popular child actor and had played sensitive teens in such legendary films as *Rebel Without a Cause*, had made the switch to directing, an art in which he excelled. He planned to direct a show about prison titled *Fortune and Men's Eyes* in Los Angeles. Mineo flew to San Francisco, saw Don in *Your Own Thing*, and immediately scheduled an audition, hiring Don on the spot after his reading.

And so Don arrived in Los Angeles, the city that was to be his blessing and his bane, in 1969, playing the victim of a brutal prison rape who ends up as animalistic as his attackers.

Don won excellent notices from the L.A. critics in the show, and soon afterward he told a reporter he credited Mineo with his success, comparing him to a sculptor who'd molded Don Johnson the actor out of rough clay. Even years later he would say, "To a great degree Sal was responsible for my success in this town. I was on stage two hours, thirty-five minutes, eight shows a week, for eight months."

When Mineo was murdered several years later, Don was hit hard by the act of violence that had snatched the life of his mentor. But even though Don was grateful to Sal for discovering him and helping him, he'd never felt he really knew the man. "Sal was an enigma," he said just last year. "He was gay, by his own admission, but I don't know that he was completely gay, because he was also with women. But he was fascinated by me and my persona."

During the making of *Rebel Without a Cause,* the teenage Mineo had idolized both his costars, Natalie Wood and James Dean. Undoubtedly, something in Don's pouty sensuality struck a chord, reminding Sal of James Dean, who hadn't been much older than Don when he died in the fiery crash of his Porsche in 1955.

Immediately after the production of *Fortune and Men's Eyes* closed, Don made a commitment to staying in Los Angeles, though Mineo would have liked him to accompany the play to New York. As it turned out, Don would be heading to New York anyhow, to play the title role in (and be in almost every single scene of) *The Magic Garden of Stanley Sweetheart*. He was sure the movie was going to be his biggest break of all.

4

The Magic Garden, The Bitter Weed

Don Johnson is hardly the kind of man to quote someone like Richard Milhous Nixon. But there's something Nixon once said which would strike a chord in Don Johnson.

"Success is not a harbor," according to the former president of the United States, "but a voyage with its own perils to the spirit. The game of life is to come up a winner, to be a success, or to achieve what we set out to do. Yet there is always the danger of failing as a human being. The lesson that most of us on this voyage never learn, but can never quite forget, is that to win is sometimes to lose."

Don won the starring role in *The Magic Garden of Stanley Sweetheart,* and at first success was sweet. It was only much later that he understood just how deeply he had lost by winning.

He was, when stardom struck, barely into his twenties, little more than a child. In *The Magic Garden of Stanley Sweetheart* he actually *looks* like a child, with his tawny hair falling into bangs, wide blue eyes, and petulant mouth. He'd graduated from high school just three years before.

Now, here he was—a star. Or so everybody told him. He was being wined and dined, interviewed, photographed, staying in posh hotel suites, driven in sleek black limousines. "I had grown up in Missouri and Kansas," he later mused, "and here I was, this young man with a movie and a lot of money, and in New York where I'd never been, and everybody at M-G-M was doing everything for me. . . . I was pampered a little too much, I guess. I started believing it all . . . got caught up in the craziness of the whole thing. It was unreal."

Overnight stardom isn't easy for anyone to take with a grain of salt. For someone Don's age, it was dangerous—and tempting. The first temptation he gave in to was failing to keep his mouth shut. Hey, all the guys at

M-G-M acted as if every word that came out of his mouth was profound, right? What was to stop him from thinking he really had something to say? "I was young, long-haired, and idealistic," he later admitted, but at the time, he was willing to wax eloquent on almost any subject under the sun. In one interview of the period, he declaimed on such serious subjects as the generation gap, war, and pollution. No subject was too deep, too worldly for the young man, who, when politics and government were brought up, blithely predicted "total revolution."

Don Johnson learned the hard way just how unimportant he was in the world's total scheme. As the bad reviews started pouring in for *The Magic Garden of Stanley Sweetheart,* M-G-M, the same studio whose "yes men" had been indulging Don's every whim a short time before, coolly informed him that they wouldn't be renewing his option for a second picture.

Don was dumbfounded. After all, the reviews hadn't suggested tarring and feathering *him*. If anything, he'd escaped relatively unscathed, with most of the criticism aimed at the film itself, which was deemed a lackluster attempt to cash in on the success of counterculture psychedelia like *Hair,* one of Broadway's biggest hits of the late 1960s.

M-G-M had talked him up. Now they were dropping him back into the same obscurity from which they'd plucked him without so much as another chance to make good. "I felt my career was over," Don recalled in a recent interview with *TV Guide*. "They had written me off. I took whatever I could find."

His taking whatever he could find wasn't restricted to acting roles. He was taking a good share of the drugs and booze that were freely dispensed in Los Angeles at the time.

The time was an era where "hip" didn't mean the Gianni Versace suits and tertiary colors of *Miami Vice*. Hip meant headbands and day-glo mandalas. Hip meant *Bonnie and Clyde, Easy Rider, Performance, Monterey Pop*, and *Woodstock*. Hip meant Cuervo Gold Tequila, *Dos Equis,* Panama Red, Columbian Gold, Bolivian Flake, and Peruvian Mother-of-Pearl. Hip meant hash from Lebanon and Nepal, cocaine from South America, marijuana from Mexico and points south. Hip meant parties that lasted for days, where nobody ever figured out exactly who was the host. Hip meant waking up after the streetlights went on and heading for the nearest party.

Los Angeles today isn't the L.A. of the early seventies. It can't afford to be. Within the past ten years or so, the gravy train just doesn't stop there the way it once did. Movie, TV, and record companies have tightened their belts and stopped throwing free parties every night of the week. The freebies cut into their inflated budgets too much.

In the early seventies, a good-looking young man or woman with the right connections could live practically for free simply by sticking with the party circuit. There were plenty of hangers-on who never worried about where their next meal or drink was coming from, not with some sort of press party (or even two, or three) going on practically every night of the week. All that mattered was knowing the right people or getting on the right "lists," and, maybe, coming up with rent and gas money. And if you were on the right lists for the record companies, even this wasn't a problem, not with twenty to fifty free LPs being delivered right to the door every week, albums that were easily exchanged for cash at one of the many stores doing a brisk business in promotional copies.

For Don, there were always plenty of parties, even when there weren't enough interviews, readings, or callbacks. In the fourteen years after *The Magic Garden of Stanley Sweetheart,* Don worked. But he didn't work enough, and what jobs he did get weren't memorable. He had plenty of free time on his hands and too many disappointments.

He did films—*Zachariah, A Boy and His Dog, Return to Macon County*. And he did television—*The Rebels, Amateur Night at the Dixie Bar and Grill, From Here to Eternity, Revenge of the Stepford Wives, Elvis and Me, Beulah Land, First You Cry, The Lives of Carol Leitner*, the occasional guest-starring spot. But nothing he did lived up to those bright promises all the studio sycophants had made when he'd signed to star in *The Magic Garden of Stanley Sweetheart*. The plum roles were going to other actors, actors who'd started out when Don had, actors nobody had heard of in 1970.

Those years of rejection left scars that may have healed but which will never fade completely, scars that may have indirectly contributed to Don's eventual real success, simply because they gave him the world-weariness that is so inherent in his portrayal of Sonny Crockett.

Just recently, he emotionally told Susan Shapiro, "I was with William Morris for five years and I had come to them as a young client with a future. When I went with them, their business was changing and I got shuffled into the back drawer. Finally, they came to me one day and suggested that I get out of the business, that I was never going to make it. *!*! you, William Morris!"

Now that he's firmly entrenched in the Hollywood heavens, Don can be upfront about what he calls the "*major* despair" of those years of rejection. Back then, he had to stay "up" for interviews, convince everyone he was still riding the crest of that first wave of success. "I'm just making my mark in the business," he said optimistically while he was filming an episode of *Barnaby Jones* in the midseventies. "I'm ornery, but I wouldn't hurt a soul. I've always enjoyed doing things with a group of people, and I enjoy this." Indicating the cast and crew of the segment, he insisted, "They like me, and I like them." But even while he was cheerfully saying that, *The City,* the latest in a long string of pilots he'd made (this one, interestingly, for NBC) was being given thumbs down.

Every time he went into a new project, Don told himself this was his chance, this was going to be the movie or TV show that was finally going to bring him the lasting fame he'd expected with *The Magic Garden of Stanley Sweetheart*. Time and time again, his hopes were dashed.

He got some satisfaction out of the fact that he was usually singled out for praise.

But praise isn't enough when the project itself is lambasted.

A case in point is 1975's *Return to Macon County*. Writer-director Richard Compton had made a hit with his *Macon County Line,* starring Max Baer, Jr., two years earlier, and sequel fever, which wouldn't peak until a few years later, was already beginning to sweep the country. So he decided why not make more of the same? For the new film, he used new actors. Nick Nolte was the star and a decent box-office draw at the time, so it seemed like a break when Don was offered second billing.

Richard Eder's review was typical. Writing in the *New York Times,* Eder dismissed the lead actors with one offhand line of applause— "Both the young men, played by Nolte and Don Johnson, are very good"—then went on to excoriate the film itself, stating that "one of the troubles with *Return to Macon County*— besides a mindless plot and its gross imitation of the atmosphere of *American Grafitti*— is that no sooner do its young protagonists begin to charm than the viewer begins to wait unhappily to see where the bullet holes will appear."

Don Johnson got used to reading a lot of reviews like that. But he kept swimming against the current that seemed to be trying to tell him he wasn't going to get anywhere. He kept talking himself up, trying to tell himself, and everybody else, that everything was just hunky-dory. "I pride myself on creating a different physical appearance for each character," he told one interviewer. "That helps build totally different performances, but it doesn't make for much recognition. I'd rather have it that way. I'd rather be a good actor than a personality."

And he kept pushing the demons away with wine, women, song, and drugs, pretending he was doing it because it was the thing to do, not because it made every new letdown more bearable. Even later he had trouble admitting the partying wasn't fun. "It was the era of 'let's get high!' " he remarked. "The very permissive, rebellious '60s and '70s when everybody was doing drugs. You'd go to a party, and if you didn't do drugs, you weren't invited. I was the type that if I had it, you had it."

Johnson didn't just go to parties, he threw them as well. His rented house in the Hollywood Hills was a well-known party spot, where Jack Nicholson, Cass Elliot, Peter Bogdanovich, or a member of the Allman Brothers Band might drop in. If he wasn't throwing a party of his own, Don might be found at Hugh Hefner's, where the partying never stopped. Or he might be on a plane, headed somewhere that had sounded like a good idea at the time: Tangiers, New York, Mexico. "I never drank or did drugs while I was working," he's said. "But, brother, when they said wrap, I would try to set the land speed record. I knew how to party, too. . . . I traveled in a crowd. I would say, 'Hey, I have an idea. Let's all go to Mexico City and have some Mexican food. Call the airport, and let's go.' "

And still, he kept trying to convince everyone he was going to make it. Even during the filming of NBC's miniseries version of *From Here to Eternity*, it was extremely doubtful that the network was going to pick it up. But Don, who was playing the newly created role of Private Robert E. Lee Prewitt's brother, spoke of the series as if it were a surefire long-term success.

"The way I finally ended up playing Prewitt," he said, "was a demonstration of synchronousity [sic]. Things happen in time and space just the way they're supposed to.

"I was committed to a pilot at ABC when they were getting ready to do the miniseries. If I'd been eligible then, I wouldn't be eligible now for what I think will be the season's most prestigious series.

"I had offers from all three networks," he

boasted. "I could have done any series I was remotely right for. But this is the only kind of role and the only kind of situation I'd want to do on a continuing basis." He went on to say that while no one could predict a hit, *From Here to Eternity* had all the right ingredients.

Back then, in 1980, all the right ingredients just weren't enough. Don Johnson would still have four long years to wait until he found a series that was the smash he'd dreamed of for so long.

In the meantime, according to Don, "They tell me I was a lot of fun to be with." A typical day of drinking meant a case of beer, a few martinis before dinner, a couple of bottles of good wine with the meal, and snifters of Napoleon brandy afterward.

When other actors one's own age and younger are getting the choice roles, the Emmy and Oscar nominations, it's easy to say the hell with it, to knock back another drink, snort another line, smoke another joint. "I just didn't have the discipline to handle failure," Don confessed to Harry F. Waters during a *Newsweek* interview in 1985. "I would look around and see actors working who were no better than I was. I mean, I started when Jeff Bridges and Timothy Bottoms and all those guys started. But for some reason, it didn't work out for me. . . ."

What could he do? He talked big ("I'm not used to playing second fiddle" was his comment on his role in *From Here to Eternity* in 1980), doggedly went to interviews only to see the really meaty roles go to other actors, and drowned his anxieties in any escape that seemed like a good idea at the time.

According to what Don told a *Rolling Stone* reporter, he was doing some outrageous things when he was coked out, even marrying for the second time—to a girl he termed "a bimbo" who "didn't do anything. She was from a wealthy family, and I thought that might be fun to do for a while. A short while—we got it annulled in a matter of days."

Still, screw-ups and all, as long as there was a party going on someplace, Don didn't have to stop to wonder what had become of the kid who'd left Wichita for the West Coast convinced he was star material. And it seemed there was always a party going on somewhere. And always a woman willing to follow as he sped along in the fast lane.

5

Pinky and Pear Play House

The folks back in Wichita say Donnie Wayne Johnson was a real ladies' man even as a teenager. His high-school girlfriend, the former Anna Davis, remembers fighting about "his flirting with women." His old buddy Jim Oaks recalls him as "a playboy."

Johnson kept to his wicked, wicked ways after arriving in Hollywood. According to Pamela Miller Des Barres, a former girlfriend who shared Johnson's digs in the early seventies, "Donnie always had the starlet of the moment. They were all at his place, and anyone could see why. He was drop-dead gorgeous. I mean, he was prettier than I was."

Women had always been easy for him to come by. That combination of cockiness and vulnerability that's become synonymous with Johnson in his *Miami Vice* role of Sonny Crockett has always been there. Like many adults who were the products of broken homes, he's still got a touch of the bruised little boy about him, certainly a factor that makes his current lady, like all the women before her, call her thirty-six-year-old lover "Donnie" and not "Don."

In the days of *The Magic Garden of Stanley Sweetheart* and afterward, Don played hard and fast, often showing up at a party with more than one date. But his fragile psyche needed more than just a steady stream of women, and he found it in someone even more vulnerable than himself.

Melanie Griffith was disoriented by the Hollywood scene as much as any newcomer, though she'd made her first TV appearance— in a commercial—at the age of nine months. She was born in New York City, the daughter of model Tippi Hedren. Melanie was just four when her mother divorced Peter Griffith, now a realtor in the Virgin Islands. She was just five when Alfred Hitchcock spotted her mother in a soap commercial, flew her to the coast for a screen test, then signed her to star in his 1963 film, *The Birds*.

In Hollywood, Melanie's life assumed the unreal quality of a child with a movie star for a mother. When Tippi was shooting *A Countess from Hong Kong,* Melanie sat on Charlie Chaplin's knee, gazed at Sophia Loren, and charmed Marlon Brando, who wrote in her autograph book, "You're a lovely lady, Melanie, and I hope to see you again and again."

One person Melanie didn't want to see at all was Alfred Hitchcock, whom she recently stated used her mother as "a puppet." The misanthropic Hitchcock gave Melanie one of the strangest birthday presents any six-year-old has ever received. He sent her a box, inside of which was a smaller, wooden box shaped like a coffin; inside that was a miniature of Tippi Hedren, laid out in a copy of the dress she'd worn in *The Birds.* "My mom," Melanie later said in what for her was an unusual understatement, "was in shock."

Melanie was still a child when her mother remarried, taking film producer Noel Marshall as her second husband (they are now divorced). Melanie spent the rest of her childhood on a two-hundred-acre ranch in Acton, California, sharing the homestead, and her mother's attention, with Marshall's three sons, a sister, and a variety of animals that included lions, tigers, and elephants.

It had to have been a strange, disjointed life for Melanie, who later said she'd had "too much, too soon." Like Don Johnson, she didn't have what might have made her happiest—her own parents living happily ever after. Peter Griffith, happy with the switch he'd made from filming commercials to selling real estate, stayed in the Caribbean, marrying again. In 1975, Melanie flew down to the islands to take care of the two children from her father's second marriage while Griffith, who was about to be divorced a second time, made a trip to Europe. "It's a better relationship than before," Melanie insisted bravely. "I didn't see him often enough." At the time, she was seeing him only three times a year.

It was while she was in her teens that Melanie began having a fantasy about Marilyn Monroe. Tippi Hedren had given birth to Melanie in New York City's Doctors' Hospital the same day Marilyn Monroe, then married to Arthur Miller, had lost her own baby there. Melanie had always been told that Marilyn had cuddled her in her arms there in the hospital for consolation; as a teenager, she decided she was really Monroe's child. "I didn't look like my mother at the time. I figured that when Marilyn held me in her arms, God had switched me over real fast."

Like Marilyn, Melanie was beautiful. Like Marilyn, she also grew up too fast, later describing herself as a teenager as having "the body of a woman, the feelings of a woman, but . . . just a headstrong baby."

The "headstrong" baby was fourteen when she met twenty-two-year-old Johnson, who was starring in *The Harrad Report* (yet another of his flop films) with her mother. It wasn't long before she was spending weekends with him, then sharing an apartment, then sharing a house.

At fifteen, she was offhandedly starting out on an acting career. She didn't consider herself at all unusual, since, "By fourteen, half of my girlfriends had had abortions."

At 5'8" and 110 pounds, with hair as tawny as the coats of her mother's beloved lions, Melanie was a natural model. "You know, I never really wanted to be an actress," she confessed at the ripe old age of seventeen. "My goal was to model, and I'm busy doing that, too, these days. I just signed with Eileen Ford, the same agency that Mom used to work for. Modeling is fun. I like putting on makeup, wearing fancy clothes, having my hair done. When I first started modeling eight months ago, I was paid $35 an hour. Now I'm up to $50, but I'm still a long way from those models drawing $150 an hour."

Melanie, young and willing to shock, discussed any personal subject with the same equanimity as she discussed her earnings. "I've flown here with my boyfriend who I've been living with for over a year," she told Bob Lardine in 1975. "The hotel where we are staying got angry at us for registering together as single people. If we had put down Mr. and Mrs., they wouldn't have cared. That's New York for you. In Hollywood, everything is loose. If you're married out there, they think you're weird."

Sometimes it seemed as if she didn't want to keep her mouth shut. During the same trip to New York, where she was publicizing her first movie role, in *Night Moves* with Gene Hackman, she told another reporter, "Do you know that breakfast for two costs thirty dollars? Lucky I'm not paying for it," then went on to wax eloquent on the subject of Don Johnson.

"I lived with him for a year, then we broke up for two months, and now we're together again," she told her bemused interviewer. "I didn't tell my father until last November. He objected completely, but I told him it was my life. He met Don last Christmas and likes him a lot. So does my mother."

Peter Griffith also objected when he heard that Melanie was doing seminude scenes not only in *Night Moves,* but also in *The Drowning Pool,* with Paul Newman and Joanne Woodward. Actually, Griffith didn't want his daughter in the movie business to begin with, but as a long-distance father, he had no choice but to resign himself to her wishes.

As for those nearly nude scenes, Melanie had no qualms about discussing them in worldly-wise tones. Musing about her role as a half-dressed nymphet in *The Drowning Pool,* she said, "I don't know why I keep getting those parts. It could have all started by my taking off my clothes in *Night Moves.* But I don't regret it. And of course, there's no scene of me completely naked. The law prohibits photographing minors that way. So when you see that girl swimming nude underneath the boat in the movie, that's not me. That's my double."

If Melanie's own nudity wasn't complete, it didn't leave much to the imagination, as she bared both her breasts and her bottom. "I had full confidence in Arthur [Penn, the director]," she explained. "He deemed it necessary, so I did it. No, I didn't consult my boyfriend or my mother about it. I make my own decisions."

Melanie did get to play a "nice" girl in *Smile,* the Michael Ritchie satire about a beauty pageant, but by then she seemed determined to shock. In an article in *Seventeen,* she told about a pageant she'd actually been in herself. "When I ended up among the ten finalists, we had to answer one question: who do you admire most? I said Barbra Streisand for her voice, Michelangelo for his art, and my boyfriend because he's the best. I figured that would disqualify me, and it worked. Because then they asked, the best at what? I didn't say anything, just walked up the ramp!"

Meanwhile, literally back at the ranch, Melanie's mother was trying to justify her daughter's precocity. When a reporter asked if she'd liked *Smile,* Tippi admitted, "I liked *Night Moves* more, but Melanie's nudity in it did bother me. I was on the set several times while it was being filmed, and I would have preferred her not doing it. But somehow the young people of today take a different view of things than we do, and than I certainly did. But I have great respect for my daughter and her talent, and I think everyone's making too much of the nudity."

Describing her child as a "fun-loving, funny,

enchanting person," Hedren tried to sound casual about her daughter's live-in lover. "It bothered me at first that she was with Donnie," she confessed. "But then again, the young people of today have much different attitudes than we did. I like Donnie very much, and I'd sooner see her having a beautiful relationship with him than going through what a lot of young girls do in unhappy dating. But I still think Melanie is too young to marry."

Years later Melanie would say ruefully, "Young girls in Hollywood can be very deceiving. You look like a woman, but you're still a child inside. If you're strong-willed, like I was, people let you get away with a lot. But in the end, it all catches up with you."

During her first few years with Don, Melanie's worries about the future were confined to her career. She'd missed out on two movie roles she'd wanted—one because she was too tall, the other, in *The Exorcist*, produced by stepfather Marshall, because she looked too old (the role eventually went to Linda Blair)—and she spoke constantly about going to college and getting an education. She said she didn't want to be "washed up at twenty without knowing anything."

For the time being, she felt she knew all

she needed to know about love. She talked about the house she and Don rented in Laurel Canyon and their Russian wolfhound Goldie with all the naive enthusiasm of a little girl playing house. She got upset when the press asked her if she was dating. Dating! Really! Why would a sixteen-year-old girl date when she was already living with the man of her dreams? As a token of her love, Melanie dropped in at Lyle Tuttle's tattoo parlor on the Sunset Strip (as many other stars, including Janis Joplin, had done) and emerged with a pear tattooed on her rump. Why a pear? Because that's what she called Donnie, who nicknamed her "Pinky" in return.

Don says he *wasn't* in love with Melanie in the beginning. From the moment he met her, she chased him, phoning him and suggesting they get together. Finally, he gave in and agreed to lunch.

But Melanie had more in mind than burgers and shakes. She seemed to have her mind made up that she was ready to lose her virginity, as so many of her friends already had—and that Don Johnson was going to be the one.

To a twenty-two-year-old who was already staring failure in the face, it was extremely flattering. At least, Don recently told *Roll-*

ing Stone, "That's the way I took it. So when it started out, it wasn't incredibly romantic— it was almost . . . uh, clinical.

"It was a special time and moment for us, but I wasn't head over heels in love with her. It was more that I gave in. I thought, 'If that's the way it's going to be, it might as well be done right as opposed to the back seat of a car with some fifteen-year-old.' "

The difference in their ages was, Don admitted, more chronological than psychological. "Melanie was very much a young lady of the world, and I was not necessarily mature. Her extreme maturity and my lack of maturity probably worked out pretty well."

Melanie celebrated her eighteenth birthday with a *Playboy* layout and interview, which featured her lover and for which she was paid $10,000. Shortly afterward, she left Johnson, not for the first time.

She did go back to him, perhaps because she didn't like life in the fast lane without a companion, or maybe because she wasn't happy with the Vietnamese refugees now living with Tippi and giving Melanie even more competition for her attention. The most likely reason, however, is that the teenager still couldn't distinguish love from infatuation.

In what she would end up referring to as

"this one mistake [that] could have ruined my life," Melanie married her Donnie. "We thought if we were married and it still didn't work, we'd divorce," she told *People* in 1985. Within a matter of months, that's exactly what they did.

Don, who's said of his relationship with Griffith, "I did feel a little strange picking her up after school," speaks of the marriage as just another one of those episodes from his own "too much, too soon" years. "I don't remember it all that clearly sometimes, those days," he says.

He does remember that he'd spent most of the night with ex–Miss World Marjorie Wallace when, shortly after he'd returned home, Melanie called at about four or five in the morning. They made up over the phone, swore "undying love," as he puts it, then flew to Las Vegas and got married.

When they split, they kept the life-style they'd pursued together. Don went back to the Playboy mansion and his string of starlets, while Melanie kept on partying, with Ryan O'Neal among others.

Their relationship, adolescent as it was, had given the two of them some sort of security neither had known before. Without one another as an anchor, they drifted along at Hollywood's frantic pace, both nearly spinning out of control. "Sure, I used to do drugs," Melanie admitted after she finally got her act together. "I used to drink. I was wild. I could do anything I wanted, and I did."

Melanie was lost, and she floundered in her attempts to build a life without Donnie. She was still getting movie roles, but now they were "B" movies, like her 1977 feature, *Joyride*. And even though she was still acting, Melanie now began to doubt her own talent. "It was said I was very good," she told the *Los Angeles Times* in 1983, "but I really didn't know what I was doing. Like my mom, it just happened to me. I didn't know what it meant to be an actress."

When Warren Beatty suggested she study with Stella Adler, Melanie headed straight for New York. But insecure and anxious, it wasn't long before she panicked and headed straight back to the coast.

She had her share of hardships to make up for her charmed youth. In 1977, while filming *Roar*, she was mauled by a lion, and still carries faint scars on her face.

Then, in 1980, the whole world came crashing down on her. In an accident she terms "kind of ironic," Melanie was run down by a drunken driver at a crosswalk on Sunset Boulevard.

She suffered serious injuries, including a broken arm and temporary amnesia, and, as she began recovering, started thinking of the accident as "God's way of telling me to slow down and figure out what to do with my life."

Shortly afterward, Melanie was filming a TV movie called *She's in the Army Now*. Her best friend, Jamie Lee Curtis, was also in the telefilm, as was a young actor named Steven Bauer, who played Curtis's boyfriend. In real life, Bauer ended up with Melanie (Johnson recently told *Playboy* he introduced the two of them, but that seems unlikely).

Bauer was dark and handsome. He was also an intense, serious actor who wanted to get better. He wanted to go to New York to study with Stella Adler. Melanie went along, and this time, with Bauer by her side for emotional support, she stuck it out.

Back in Los Angeles, it wasn't easy. Though she'd gotten her weight back down to 110 pounds (from 130) after the accident, she still wasn't getting good parts. Her past had caught up with her, and she knew she was losing jobs because of the way people remembered her.

When her agent wanted to send her out for a role on a TV series, Melanie refused and was told, "You can't take that kind of attitude. You're nothing, and don't forget it." Melanie left the agency, but she couldn't help wondering if her career was going to stay on the skids.

Like Don Johnson had in the past, Melanie kept talking optimistically, telling one reporter, "If I work now, I know it's because I'm good and not because I'm the new kid on the block." But what if she didn't get the chance to show people?

In 1982, she married Bauer in St. Patrick's Cathedral. Shortly before meeting him, Melanie had joined a self-help group for alcoholics, and now, with her husband's help, she came to terms with her problems. "I was very stubborn about being confronted with talk that I was an alcoholic or a drug addict," she admitted. "You don't want to face it, but once you do, it's like a hundred pounds is lifted off your chest."

Considering herself "one of the lucky ones" to have gotten off the treadmill of drugs and alcohol, Melanie sought work with renewed vigor. She was willing to take chances to prove she was dependable and could act.

Her husband's career was on the move, with *Scarface* and *Thief of Hearts*. And now, instead of fighting against the sexy roles she'd once feared would typecast her forever, she went after them, deciding she could bring "a lot of life to that kind of character." She played a stripper involved in a lesbian affair and drugs in *Fear City*, then fought for the role of "Holly Body" in Brian De Palma's *Body Double*.

Interestingly enough, De Palma was probably one of the few directors in Hollywood who'd never given Melanie black marks for promiscuity, because when she had auditioned for *Carrie*, she balked at necking with an actor during the reading, telling him she just couldn't kiss someone she didn't know! De Palma had to tell her to forget the part.

Melanie eventually won the *Body Double* role. In the film, a parody of Hollywood disguised as a mystery, she played a star of X-rated movies (beating out several "adult" film actresses, including Annette Haven, for the part) who's unwittingly used to commit a murder. Melanie walked away with the movie. Even critics who disliked the film itself singled her out for praise.

Like Don, Melanie has picked up the pieces of her life, living happily with Bauer, whom she calls "Rocky," in West Hollywood, where, in August of 1985, she gave birth to a five-pound, eight-ounce boy. She talks about going to school at UCLA and appearing one day on stage opposite her husband. The play she'd most like to do is *Born Yesterday*, which is something no one ever accused Melanie Griffith of being.

6

"Meet Number Four!"

While Melanie was spinning out of control in the late seventies, Don Johnson was dealing with some major demons of his own. Not yet thirty, he'd just divorced his third wife. His career was going no place but down. And his mother died.

Nell Johnson was just forty-two when she lost her battle against lymph-gland cancer in 1975. She'd had the disease for a year, but before that, her health had been seriously undermined by alcoholism. Don tried to do everything he could for her—getting her off alcohol, making sure she ate properly, even paying to send her to a laetrile clinic in

Mexico. But it was too late to save her. The last time Don returned to Wichita was for her funeral; he hasn't been back since.

His mother's death was one more reason to keep the party going, to not face up to the despair that was never farther away than arm's reach.

Don no longer fooled himself into thinking he didn't have a problem. "I knew it instinctively," he recently told a *Rolling Stone* interviewer. "It doesn't take a f—ing genius to realize that if you get f—ed up on Thursday and Friday, Saturday and Sunday, have to recover on Monday and Tuesday, leaving the only day you have left for work Wednesday, then you're an addictive personality. But, still," he insisted, "my drug usage wasn't as bad as the press has built it up to be—I wasn't one of those people who blew fortunes—and yet it wasn't as tame as to be insignificant. . . ."

Just as every cloud has some sort of silver lining, Don's background in the drug scene has a positive side: he uses his past experiences to act as an informal adviser on *Miami Vice*'s dope-dealing scenes. "Whenever I see something that doesn't jibe," he once explained, "I'll say, 'Wait a minute, guys, this isn't the way it goes down.' They know that I know, and they respect my opinion."

Though he was never actually a dealer, Johnson says he "knew all of it." Part of this is a result of his predilection for hanging out with people who play fast and loose with society's mores, for finding "the social misfits and the thieves the most interesting." During the first season of *Miami Vice,* Don eagerly accepted an invitation to visit the two-hundred-acre Florida compound of a reputed crime-syndicate boss. "It fit right in with my idea of a good time," he told *Newsweek*'s Harry F. Waters. "It made my heart thump a little faster and all my senses a little sharper."

It was during the late seventies that he started hanging out with the Allman Brothers, growing especially close to band member Dicky Betts, still a friend today. Don put his songwriting talents to use with the Allmans, cowriting two of the songs on the *Enlightened Rogues* album—"Blind Love" and "Can't Take It with You." The album ended up going gold.

In the meantime, the fun of nonstop partying was wearing thin, but Don had nothing with which to replace it. The challenging roles that might make the world sit up and take notice of Don Johnson weren't coming his way. But the drinks and drugs, and, of course, the women were.

"One time I saw a girl in San Francisco," Don reminisced with Susan Shapiro, "and we were shooting on the streets. She was a stone-cold knockout beauty. She was walking by me, and you can tell when someone looks at you if it's mutual. I stopped her and grabbed her hands and said, 'You have beautiful hands. Do you play the piano?' She said no, and I said, 'Do you——?' She said sometimes. And that started it, right there."

That's how it was with Don—the women were always easy to find, easy to replace.

And then he ran into Patti D'Arbanville at Mr. Chow's.

Patti D'Arbanville's childhood was as typically New York as Johnson's was midwestern. Born in Manhattan, she'd grown up in the laid-back atmosphere of Greenwich Village, where her father was a bartender and her mother an artist. She started attracting attention when she was only three, when her grandmother took her to Bloomingdale's and entered her in their beautiful baby contest, which she won.

"I went on to being an Ivory Soap baby for television commercials," she says, "and for three years I sat in a bathtub and said either, 'And it floats,' or, 'Get some today.'"

By the time she was thirteen, she was working at the Café Figaro on Bleecker

Street, putting go-go records on the turntable—a notable job mainly because the Figaro had no cabaret license and, therefore, no dancing. It gained fame as the home of "sit down" dancing, as expresso-drinking teens overcame the legal barriers by dancing in their seats.

A year later, she quit school. "I was bright. I was always ahead of the others, but somehow I never thought I needed school." What she needed was excitement, and she found it with Andy Warhol and his friends.

Pop artist Warhol met Patti while she was plying her diskette trade at the Figaro. "I started hanging out with the Warhol crowd. I was very young, it seemed like an awful lot was going on, and I was seeing a slice of life I hadn't seen before. Warhol wanted to put me in a film, but my mother wouldn't let me."

Happily, her mother had no objections a short time later when Patti decided to become a model. She was working at Mickey Ruskin's Max's Kansas City on Park Avenue South, a favorite hangout of the Warhol gang at the time (and just a stone's throw from the Warhol "Factory"). One customer was fashion illustrator Antonio Lopez, who'd often sit at one of the red-tableclothed booths and sketch the pretty young waitress. One

73

night he suggested she try her hand modeling, since she had such a pretty face in spite
of the fact that she was rather short, at 5′4″,
to be a model.

She went straight to Wilhemina, one of
the top agencies, which signed her after looking at test shots by the top photographers
like Richard Avedon, Bert Stern, and Fran-
cesco Scavullo (who later included Patti in
his book, *Scavullo, On Beauty*). "Sexy, small,
and feminine" were the words Scavullo used
to describe the fashion world's new discovery. Years later, the words still apply.

In 1968, when she was just seventeen, Patti
headed for Europe, modeling in France, En-
gland, West Germany, and Italy, staying overseas for five years off and on. In London, she
was approached for a leading role in *La
Maison*, a French film starring Michel Si-
mon. The fact that she wasn't fluent in the
language didn't faze her—she simply spent
six hours a day for the next two months
studying with a tutor, until she spoke French
like a native—and got the part. The film,
though no box-office smash, was a critical
success. And Patti D'Arbanville was hooked
on acting.

She continued modeling between film jobs,
most of which were French-speaking. She
appeared in *The Crazy American Girl*, David

Hamilton's *Bilitis, La Saignée,* and Andy Warhol's *L'Amour.* Her role was a lot bigger than it had been when she'd worked with other "Factory" people like Viva and Joe D'Allesandro in John Schlesinger's *Midnight Cowboy* back in '68. Then, she'd been just an extra.

Though she was doing well in Europe, she came back to the States after five years because "I wasn't getting the parts I wanted and I wanted to stop modeling totally. I wanted to come back to the United States to try my luck." In New York, she studied acting with Herbert Berghof. Then, late in 1973, she headed for California.

Though already well known in Europe, Patti didn't exactly take Hollywood by storm. She spent some time working at Maxfield Blue, a chic boutique, where she waited on stars (once selling Barbra Streisand a half-dozen cashmere sweaters) while waiting for her break.

She started getting small but good parts. In *Rancho Deluxe,* directed by Frank Perry, she got to work with seasoned pros like Jeff Bridges, Elizabeth Ashley, and Sam Waterston. She played Bridges' girlfriend, a beer-drinking rodeo barrel-racer.

In Paris working on a picture, she met Roger Mirmont, a French stage actor, marrying him in 1975. Patti then started trying to have a transcontinental marriage, commuting between Los Angeles and Paris. The situation imposed a strain on both her career and her marriage, but Mirmont wasn't happy with her suggestion that he move to California. After two years of marriage, the Mirmonts separated and Patti rented an apartment in Venice, California, overlooking the Pacific and close to the Venice skateway, where she roller-skated about twelve miles each day.

She continued to get good supporting roles in feature films: *Time After Time, Big Wednesday, The Main Event,* and *Modern Problems.* In *The Main Event,* she played fighter Ryan O'Neal's floozy girlfriend, a role she was given by the woman to whom she'd once sold sweaters, Barbra Streisand.

Patti was famous in that film for her incredible cough, and it was that cough that won her the role. When she was auditioning for Streisand, Patti had a chest cold and couldn't help coughing. "I let out this enormous cough, and she [Streisand] roared and said, 'That's great coming out of this little body. We've got to use it.'"

She was in danger of being typecast as a dizzy blonde when she got the part of Chevy Chase's "perfect" wife in *Modern Problems.*

She was immediately drawn to the part, explaining, "There's a lot of imperfection in humanity, so I tried to play her very human. She's loyal, loving, and true, but very independent." Those words might have been penned for the real-life role Patti would soon be playing as Don Johnson's girlfriend.

Patti and Don had first met years before, when he was in New York filming *The Magic Garden of Stanley Sweetheart*. Don was being shown around Warhol's Factory, where Patti was posing nude. Don says the first impression "registered," but he didn't see Patti until several years later when he was married to Melanie and Patti was married to Mirmont (who was her second husband).

Don, who says Patti was "really wild and always loud" in those days, ran into her once again later. Only, this time, though both were divorced, he was with another woman.

The next time they happened to bump into each other, Don was dating Tanya Tucker. Tanya and Don had taken a limo to the races for the day, but he'd sent her into Mr. Chow's chic Rodeo Drive Chinese restaurant alone while he took the limousine home. By the time he returned to Mr. Chow's, Tanya was surrounded by a crowd, busily holding court.

Not wanting to get involved in that scene, Don took a seat at the bar, where, he later recalled, "Though I didn't see Patti, who was at a table with friends, she saw me. Later she sent her friends home and joined me at the bar. . . ."

The rest of that story is already becoming part of the Don Johnson legend. The two were having a few drinks and chatting casually when she asked, "Weren't you married?" When Don answered in the affirmative, she asked, "How many times have you been married?" After he told her three, she announced, "Well, say hello to number four!"

Her aggressive approach worked, since, in Don's words, "She moved in that night, and we stayed in bed for about eight days. The houseboy kept bringing food and water."

Today, Don calls Patti his best friend and says, "I trust her implicitly. She unconditionally cares about me and I about her. We have the obvious problems that come from any kind of relationship, only ours are a little more public. But one reason we're able to maintain our relationship is that we're not married. A lot of times, in a marriage, you end up living someone else's idea of what it's supposed to be like, some storybook thing. As I said about partying, I've partied. I've also been married."

So Patti hasn't yet become "number four," but Don's been faithful to her in his fashion since that night at Mr. Chow's. "Patti is the dearest, most thoughtful person in the whole world," he told *People*. "That's why I love her so much."

When Patti and Don hooked up, both were still *major* party people. Then something happened just three months after the two started living together that changed everything. Patti discovered she was pregnant.

"Patti had always been told she couldn't have children," Don told Nancy Collins. "Suddenly she got very sick, and they thought she had a tubal pregnancy. But they went in and discovered it was in the wall, was a pregnancy. When she came to [from the operation], I said, 'What do you want to do?' and she said, 'There's no question about it. I'm having this baby.' I said, 'Well, where does that put us? Because I don't want to get married.' And she said, 'You don't have to marry me. I'm not into that.' So I said, 'Fine, Let's roll.' . . . We both had been major party people, but she stopped drinking, smoking, stopped using drugs. Jesse was born nine pounds and seven ounces."

Jesse Wayne was born December 7, 1982, a Sagittarius like his daddy. Patti, who'd gotten involved in a program to drop drugs

79

and alcohol, stuck with her new, healthy way of life. But Don was still playing—and playing hard. Of his long-term drug and liquor abuse, he's said that "during a two- or three-year period, starting around 1979, it was out of control. I was still in control of my faculties, but I was out of control of alcohol."

One reason Don so clearly prizes Patti is that she stuck by him during the bleaker days of his life. But it was hard for her, and she had contemplated leaving him. "I was watching this beautiful and talented man spin out," she recalls, "and I thought that maybe the only way to help was to leave him."

It was Don who finally made the decision on his own to get his life together. "I walked into the breakfast room one morning," he told *People,* "and the sun was shining and the birds were singing and Patti was feeding the baby. I came staggering in and sat down and looked at them, and she looked at me and I knew that if I didn't do something she was going to leave. So I said, 'Patti, I'm a drunk and a drug addict and I'm going to do something about it.' "

Not long before Patti had awakened to find Don sitting at a table in their Santa Monica bungalow, making notes of their possessions and how much he could get for them—so much for the stereo . . . so much for the couch . . . so much for the Caddie. . . . Don was planning to pack it all in. Disgusted with himself and his failure to make it to the top in Hollywood, he was considering selling all he'd managed to accumulate, moving back to his native state, and becoming a farmer. "I thought I should see what it was like to live a productive life," he later admitted. "Missouri? I probably would have lasted there about twenty minutes."

Patti knew Don would be taking his problems with him wherever he went. "We don't have to do that," she told him. "All we have to do is clean it up. . . . You have to start taking care of yourself."

It was on September 11, 1983, that Don decided to take her advice. For forty-five days, he went to two A.A. meetings a day, a practice that isn't uncommon with new members, "and obviously it helped. It changed my life."

Don knew the time had come for him to clean up his act, not only because it was threatening to destroy him, but because it had long ago stopped being fun. "I was miserable. I knew my life was not working, knew a long time before I quit that if I didn't get a grip on things, I'd have no career, no future.

I was probably going to kill myself with my abuses. Then my son Jesse was born, and I finally got bored, bored with the life-style, the people, the bullshit that goes with it. . . ."

In 1985, Don, in a *Newsweek* interview, said gossip columnists had blown out of proportion the importance of his feelings for his girlfriend and child in his decision to seek rehabilitation. "The actual truth," he said, "is that I quit drugs and booze because they started to bore the pants off me, and I can tolerate almost anything except being bored. If I had to sit through one more drunken cocaine rap, where me and my buddies would solve the problems of the world and the next day not remember any of it, I'd probably throw up."

Living a clean life wasn't easy, not after all those years when the partying life-style was second nature. Still, Don did it, and he feels he's learned from the years of abuse. "Ultimately, what I realized was not to feed an insecurity by going along with the masses. Looking for acceptance by doing what everybody else was doing—no matter how destructive—was not intelligent. They were all lemmings, going over the cliff, so I went with them. Luckily, before I went completely over the edge, I saw they were lemmings and I was an individual. I was lucky. But even after I quit using, it took me about eighteen months to shake down from that way of life," he said last year. "So it's only in the past six months that I feel I'm becoming the person I was meant to be. I always felt there was this person in there, waiting to emerge from behind all these obstacles, some self-imposed, some from extraneous sources."

At first, Don's abstinence didn't even touch his career, though he was also working out and running four miles a day to get back in shape. He knew he'd have to work against his reputation. "I had pretty much killed my career [by letting] my body get out of shape from drugs and alcohol," he said. "When I would go out for roles, they would say, 'I think he's had it—let's bring in the relief pitcher.' "

But he wasn't going to give up, not when he'd come so close to chucking it all. And Patti was by his side giving him support. "She was bright, intelligent, funny, interesting, and busted me from the get-go," Don once said, explaining his attraction. "I mean, to this day—three thousand miles away from each other—I can be thinking something or doing something and she'll call and say, 'Uh-huh. Yeah. I got it. You're blah, blah, blah.' And I always say, 'How did you know that?" But she just knows. Our relationship is another of those fated things. We were bound to be together—just like Jesse was sent to save both our lives. It was in the cards."

Don's attitude was very different now from what it had been in the past—a plaque on the wall of the Santa Monica bungalow he was sharing with Patti and Jesse optimistically commanded, "When life gives you lemons, make lemonade."

Don was ready to start over, to make up for his past transgressions. With the woman he loved and his son, he was rebuilding his life and his physical health. And yet that specter of defeat was never far out of sight. Though he knew he was, to a large degree, lucky, since he'd always made a living as an actor from the day he arrived in Hollywood, never having to wait tables or pump gas to make ends meet, the harsh truth was that he'd passed his thirtieth birthday without living up to the hype of *The Magic Garden of Stanley Sweetheart* days. It's a tribute to Johnson's determination and strength that he didn't lapse back into his old ways once the award-caliber roles weren't forthcoming. But he'd come too far spiritually and psychologically to go back to that mad, endless round of partying. All he could do now was hang in there and hope he'd be given one more chance to prove himself.

7

Last Chance Saloon

Don Johnson will never forget his introduction to *Miami Vice*. An actor friend telephoned him about a show in development over at Universal, something called *Dade County Fast Lane*. At the time, Don was "basically, vegetating, sitting around Hollywood like a lot of actors, waiting for the phone to ring." As soon as his friend called him, Don put in a call to his agent, asking him to get in touch with Universal and check out this *Dade County* program (Dade County is the Florida county in which Miami is located).

At first, Universal knew nothing about

86

the project. But Don's agent finally tracked the show down and got a copy of the script. As soon as Don read it, he said, "God, this is *it*. This guy's been following me around. This is my life."

These were the pre–Michael Mann days, but Don managed to get in touch with Anthony Yerkovich. They met, and Don read the writer a few scenes. When he'd finished, Yerkovich asked, "Do you understand this character that well, or are you that good?" Don answered, "Well, it's my job to make it look easy, but, yeah, I know this guy."

As soon as the meeting ended, Don telephoned his agent to tell him, "I'm going after this one. I'm going to do whatever I have to to get it."

After a few weeks had passed with nothing happening, Don decided he'd better accept the leading role he'd been offered in *Cease Fire,* a low-budget film that would be shooting in Florida. He knew that, for him, the police series was a long shot. He was pretty much considered *persona non grata* over at NBC because of the string of failed pilots he'd done for them.

In February, shooting *Cease Fire* in Miami, he got a call from Yerkovich, who was in town working on a rewrite. The two got together, and Don's hopes were kindled when he learned the leads had not yet been cast.

Back in Los Angeles, Yerkovich was trying to get people to listen when he said, "This guy Don Johnson is Sonny Crockett." Brandon Tartikoff listened. But the network executives were otherwise inclined. "Yeah, we know," they'd tell Yerkovich. "Now, who else have we got here?"

Finally, the executives agreed to take a look at a screen test, a videotape, which Don had always hated "because they're so sterile." Ordinarily, he would have issued a flat "no," but convinced he had a shot at the role, he bent his personal rule and mailed them the test. He was more convinced than ever that *Miami Vice* was for him; he thought it was the best pilot script he'd ever seen. And if there was one thing Don Johnson had seen plenty of in his checkered years in the acting business, it was pilot scripts.

He wanted to play Sonny Crockett as much as he'd ever wanted to play any character in his life, and, in debt when he started filming *Cease Fire,* he yearned for the financial security a regular series could bring.

"When the opportunity came along, I said, 'This is it,' " Don told *USA Today* about his fight for the part of Crockett. "If I had fallen

Don exuding the cool-guy charm of his "Miami Vice" character.

At the
Senior Prom.

*From the
1967 Wichita
High School
yearbook . . .*

Don as Tony in
"West Side Story."

In 1975 Don co-starred with Nick Nolte and Robin Mattson in "Return to Macon County." (courtesy of Memory Shop)

One sex symbol portrays another — Don as Elvis Presley in the 1981 NBC-TV movie, "Elvis and the Beauty Queen." (courtesy of Memory Shop)

Don played a restless youth in the film "Zachariah." (courtesy of Memory Shop)

A string of women marked Don's early Hollywood years.

1970 — Christina Clark.
(© Frank Edwards, Fotos International)

1971 — Liz Renay
(© Frank Edwards, Fotos International)

1979 — Don's sister, Jaime Skylar
(© Frank Edwards, Fotos International)

1973 — former wife Melanie Griffith
(© Frank Edwards, Fotos International)

Johnson credits actress and steady woman Patti D'Arbanville as the impetus for turning his life around.
(© Frank Edwards, Fotos International)

(© Frank Edwards, Fotos International)

TV's first super-chic cop strikes a pose with cast members Philip
Michael Thomas, Saundra Santiago, and Olivia Brown.
(© 1985 Ron Galella)

Even Duran Duran and Power Station band members are fans
of today's top TV idol. (© 1985 Ron Galella)

An expensive designer jacket, tee-shirt, and slight stubble are Don's trademarks. (© 1985 Ron Galella)

Despite the macho image, Don is a devoted and loving father to his son Jesse. (© Photoreporter, Inc.)

The handsome hunks of "Miami Vice."
(courtesy of Memory Shop)

on my face, toots, it would have been all over. This was the last-chance saloon."

By the time *Cease Fire* finished shooting, there was still no word on *Vice*. Don, trying to keep his mind off the prospect of yet another rejection, went fishing with his pal Dicky Betts.

But he couldn't get away from Sonny Crockett. He got a ship-to-shore call from his agent telling him to get back to land and then to get himself to Los Angeles pronto. NBC wanted a meeting.

"For God's sake, I've met with those guys," Don said disgustedly. "They've got more film on me than Gary Cooper. Tell them to pull something."

But his agent was adamant. They didn't want to see more footage on Don, he said. They wanted to make sure he was alive, well, and sober.

At Universal—where by now *everyone* had heard of the series—Don read with several different actors who were after the part of Tubbs, Crockett's partner. Then Philip Michael Thomas was brought in. Universal television talent VP Milt Hamerman asked the actors if they'd like to rehearse for a couple of minutes, but both shook their heads. What was happening, according to Thomas, was "BAM! That instant thing. The explosion hap-

89

pened and it was like two wild animals. And I told him, 'You're gonna need me, bud-dy!' There was that thing, that man thing."

Don felt the same chemistry, he says, and his initial impression was that Philip Michael Thomas would be someone good to work with. "He was a more than competent actor, which pleased me, and he had a lot of energy, which I felt would be a good foil for Sonny Crockett—and he was hungry. We were both hungry. It was our time. Philip knew that from the get-go. I didn't. I'd been at this altar too many times, brother. But Philip said, 'Man, don't worry about it. This is happening.' "

Don wasn't convinced, especially not when he was asked to do a film test the next day. "What do they think they're doing," he wondered, "*The Making of the President?*"

But he agreed to be tested yet again—and he got the part of Sonny Crockett, exulting, "At least I've got a role that fits me," one for which Patti D'Arbanville lightly says Don's "done the research."

Shooting the first episode was a heady experience for Johnson and Thomas, and their relationship to each other offscreen almost immediately began to echo their partnership as Crockett and Tubbs. "We had a long conversation while doing the pilot," Don told

Playboy. "We were sitting in my Miami hotel suite for a couple of hours. It was twilight. We had a view of the bay, and we were talking about how beautiful the city was and about spiritual things. We both knew what was at hand and what kinds of pressure we were going to deal with. We knew that people would be jealous of our relationship—on and off screen—be threatened by it and want to tear it apart. So we agreed that the moment either one of us felt slighted—which is never going to happen—we would discuss it. From then on, we knew that we had to be not only friends but each other's protector. And part of that protection is to allow ourselves the space we need after spending eighteen hours on the set. We don't pressure each other to have dinner together or to meet each other's families. We could ask, but we wouldn't demand it."

Philip Michael Thomas also recalled good vibes from that long discussion. "We also trained with each other," he said. "I told Don about my goal, EGOT, which stands for Emmy, Grammy, Oscar, Tony—I want to win or be nominated for each award in the next five years. And he told me about dreams he wanted to develop. So we made an effort to work out together, to jog together before the sun rose, to learn our lines together. We trained with policemen in undercover work. Don knows a lot more about guns than I do, so he taught me about weapons. During the making of the pilot, we practically lived together. We worked on Saturdays and Sundays—and you don't get *paid* for those days. And we always gave each other space, because we didn't want to force a relationship. We just wanted to be together so we could find out how we functioned. We didn't have to, but we knew this was our shot."

Thomas, who was born in Columbus, Ohio, and raised in California, was no newcomer to the business, though he was even less well known than Johnson. After sixteen years as an actor, he was well aware that *Miami Vice* had all the earmarks of being the big break he'd been waiting for.

Though they're both the same height (5'11") and almost the identical weight (at 170 pounds, Don's got five pounds on his costar), the two actors came from different worlds.

Thomas is a family-oriented man whose brother George today works as his bodyguard. He was a theology student at Oakwood College in Huntsville, Alabama, and then at the University of California at both Riverside and Berkeley until he saw the musical *Hair* (back around the same time Johnson was starting off as a movie star with *The*

Magic Garden of Stanley Sweetheart). At nineteen, that was the show he made his professional debut in, with the San Francisco company. He worked frequently enough to be known as an "up and coming" actor—guest appearances on television shows like *Good Times, Starsky and Hutch, Medical Center,* movies like *Sparkle* (opposite Irene Cara) and *Book of Numbers,* but the name Philip Michael Thomas wasn't a household word.

Then along came the role of Ricardo Tubbs, and Thomas, who'd shied away from series in the past, went after it wholeheartedly. "It was the first time I wanted to be involved with television," he told *Jet* magazine, explaining that one couldn't compare *Vice* with other series (and backing up Michael Mann's "minimovie" theory).

Don Johnson, on the other hand, once described himself as "one of the few actors who liked television." He likes the pressure, the high-pitched fast-timing, and as he said back in 1980, he still believes that "there's so much talent around these days and so few movies that *I'd* want to do that television seems the only answer for someone who wants to make a living out of acting." Back in 1980, he put his "philosophy of TV" in a nutshell. "Will Rogers was once asked why he wanted to be on radio. His answer was:

'Radio is too big to stay out of.' That's how I feel about television."

Shortly before the first episode of *Miami Vice* aired, Don spoke with *TV Guide*'s Michael Leahy in Miami, musing about how the series could affect him.

"I can walk around in Miami now, and nobody really recognizes me," he said. "That will probably change if the show does well. People will want to know about the show, and me, and Philip. I know that, I just don't want stories that say, 'He came back from a *serious* problem,' you know?" In order to keep whispering about his past at a minimum, Don decided to be upfront about his drug and alcohol abuse.

But even Don couldn't spend too much time worrying about how his future would deal with his past. Like everyone else involved in *Miami Vice*, he was more concerned with the here and now of shooting a series that caused producer John Nicolella to nickname himself "Captain Chaos" and to reply, when asked if the series was tough to make, "Tough? It's impossible."

Shooting a series on location was trouble enough. The renovated facilities used for interiors at South Florida's Fusion Studios were antiquated, dating back to the days when *Flipper* was shot there. Three art directors were given their walking papers for not coming up with the right "look." The makeup room had to be housed in an oversized closet due to space problems.

When the crew moved out of doors, there were even more problems. "The weather changes from moment to moment here," bemoaned associate producer Patti Kent. "There's a huge downpour that lasts only a minute, but when the sun comes out, everything is wet."

Some weeks, it seemed as if there was one catastrophe after another. When the crew was shooting at a run-down residential hotel, drunks kept wandering into camera range, causing scenes to be reshot. During a shooting in Puerto Rico, Philip Michael Thomas needed six stitches when a flowerpot came crashing down on his skull. When filming a speedboat chase, a jet of water nearly knocked the camera crew's helicopter into the Atlantic. Elvis the twelve-foot alligator developed a troublesome habit of slipping away—and into Biscayne Bay.

Sometimes it was all laughable, such as the scene where Sonny Crockett tackled Noogie, played by Charlie Barnett. As Don Johnson yelled, "Give me back the sixty bucks, you worm!" he tackled Barnett, throwing him to the sidewalk and pulling three twenty-dollar bills from his pocket.

Before either of the actors knew what was happening, a little old lady who'd been waiting for a bus in the seedy South Beach neighborhood started shaking a finger at Johnson and shouting, "Give him back his money! Give him back his money!" She thought she was witnessing a robbery right there in the street.

"We had a lot of explaining to do," Don said, laughing. "The woman was apparently too nearsighted to notice the camera setup behind me, and she was still mad when it was all over. With loads of location work down here, it's street theater all the way."

With twenty exteriors per show, the weird incidents will probably continue; just last year, a recent shoot had to be interrupted when a murder-robbery took place at a nearby convenience store. But at least, after the show was established as a hit during its first season, the people of Miami started coming around.

At first, the *Miami Vice* cast and crew weren't exactly welcomed with open arms. Miami didn't think its new TV status was going to be good for its image, and one group of citizens even petitioned NBC, trying to get the name of the program changed. *Miami Vice,* they thought, sounded unsavory and could hardly do much for tourism.

Besides the petitioners, there were others who didn't have the greatest things to say about the show. Actor José Ferrer, a Miami resident and director of the prestigious Coconut Grove Playhouse, said, "It's very well produced, but I think it presents one side of Miami, not the total picture. I would hate for viewers to think this is all there is to Miami—racing cars, guns, and fists."

Perhaps the biggest blow came when Metro-Dade County Police Lieutenant Pete Cuccaro quit his job as technical adviser in July, blasting the scripts with words like "demeaning," "insulting," and "totally unrealistic."

"I have no hard feelings toward the production," Cuccaro told the *Los Angeles Times* not long after he resigned. "But when it became evident that there was a great difference between the assurances I was given and the way they were ultimately carried out, I was left with no choice but to disassociate myself from a show that could be a catalyst to tear down the image of a police department we've spent four years trying to rebuild."

Cuccaro was quickly replaced by Commander Nelson Ramos of the Dade County Police Department, and the production staff swung into high gear to spread the word that *Miami Vice* had a good relationship with the police and that the Dade County Police Department was even allowing them to use its official green and white patrol cars and uniforms.

As for Cuccaro, Yerkovich said, "This is a guy who's looking for ink. All he was concerned with was a public-relations angle. If he had his way, the show would look like a cross between *Dragnet* and a Dade County Jaycees promotional film."

Yerkovich insisted the producers had explained to the city officials they weren't "trying to do *Scarface II*," which, interestingly enough, was the very film Michael Mann picked to explain the type of cable programming (*Scarface* with Al Pacino) that made all network police shows except *Miami Vice* look passé. (Also, both *Miami Vice* stars have stated that they liked *Scarface,* especially the drug rip-off and chain-saw murder that was shot at a South Beach hotel on Ocean Avenue.)

Everyone breathed a sigh of relief when Miami Beach Mayor Malcolm Feinberg said he was "pleased" with the show after seeing the pilot episode, which "shows the reality of life in the big city."

The reality of life for the *Miami Vice* company was suddenly heavy promotions chores—to make the series a hit with the residents of the city. Don and Philip started showing up at just about every charity event they could fit into their schedules (and still continue to do so). Production executives made sure everyone got the message as to how much of the million-dollar-plus-per-episode price tag went to boost the area's economy. And everyone managed to say, well, questionable things about Miami in positive terms. "This is probably the most exciting urban center in America," Michael Mann enthused, adding, "Wherever there's this much money floating around, you can always be sure there's going to be plenty of action."

The unpredictability of the entire arrangement was just fine with Johnson, who'd always relished working under pressure, anyhow. "Here's the thing: our show will never be the same every week," he excitedly told one interviewer. "Which is one of the reasons I love it. We don't have a formula. The problem is trying to tell the story from beginning to middle to end in an hour without losing the human aspect. The character bits and studies. The relationships."

Though critics found it hard to resist wordplay, one of them referring to *Vice* as a "clothes and robbers" show, the premiere was praised, even downright acclaimed. And with critical acceptance came greater acceptance by the community itself. "I like *Miami Vice*," Miami Mayor Maurice Ferre said. "It shows Miami's beauty." And in 1985, William Cullom, President of the Greater Miami Chamber of Commerce, said of the series, "It has built an awareness of Miami in young people who never thought of visiting Miami."

The show worked, not as a deterrent to tourism as folks had feared, but as an absolute, total *lure*. Miami had never looked as good as it did in *Miami Vice*'s opening credits, which dwelled not on the retirees or the impoverished emigrants but on the bikinied beauties, the crystalline waters, the racetrack, the skyline. As one writer remarked, that opening montage alone was like a weekly free commercial for the Florida Division of Tourism. Today the producers no longer worry about Miami rejecting *Miami Vice*. "I think we've become like the Miami Dolphins," Michael Mann crowed at the end of the first season. "We're the home team."

With the support of the city behind them, the *Miami Vice* team could go on to worrying about what loomed as a potential problem greater than any others in the weeks after the series' premiere. *Miami Vice* was a critical success, sure. But what in the world were they going to do about their ratings, which were completely unimpressive?

8

Vice Is Nice

Early in that first season, the praise network and production executives heaped upon
the new series sounded curiously like ratio-
nalizations, like bravado. "This show has got
a future," insisted NBC programming vice-
president Jeff Sagansky. "When people look
back in ten years, it will be a show like *Hill
Street Blues* that really stylistically changed
TV."

Meanwhile, Anthony Yerkovich was announcing, "We don't want gratuitous music-
video footage any more than we want gratuitous violence. But we do want to try and
use a more adventurous camera technique,

102

which we feel can comment on the action, accelerate the drama, and create a special mood that you're just not accustomed to seeing on network television."

And producer Michael Mann chimed in, saying, "I think the show is doing pretty good," as he insisted the ratings problem was no big deal. "The network is very happy with us because every week—except for last Friday by half a point—we've beaten *Matt Houston*. That's really our target."

From the start, Mann made himself more accessible than most executive producers. The show had become his baby, thanks to the look and sound and style he'd imposed upon it. Now he was going to make sure people wanted to watch it. "We're not MTV, we don't introduce music," he insisted, as if trying to convince parents the show wasn't just for their rock-crazy teenagers. He wanted everyone to know the montages and the drama were being integrated, while the music would always underscore the story line. "I don't want the show to be segregated into 'here's talk' and 'here's action' with some music thrown in," he averred.

Slowly but surely, the show started climbing its way up from the depths of the ratings, and there's no doubt that the massive PR campaign combined with word of mouth until everyone wanted to see *Miami Vice* at least once, just to check out what all the fuss was about. "The show definitely has more appeal to young men than the competition," said Miami radio personality Janet Cowan in a show of support. "Don Johnson and Philip Michael Johnson are real men, macho, and they are action figures. Men can relate to them."

Women could relate to them, too, because of the sensitivity of the characters, a sensitivity that's continued to develop with time. Don says, "It's something I didn't plan in having happen. I also didn't plan on everyone's picking up on it, but people did. I have gotten very bored with traditional male relationships—no touching, no holding, no genuine closeness, none of that stuff that might be misconstrued, you know. And that's the way most actors have portrayed them [men]—out of fear. I have no fear of that, so I can allow myself to be as close, open, vulnerable, weak, or gentle as possible toward my partner or friends. And I'm gratified that people have begun to pick up that it's OK for men to be close without thinking they're light in their loafers."

While it's strange for someone who's not homophobic to use his negative, old high-school expression when discussing gay men (an expression, by the way, which is as stereotypical as the image of the macho man Don says he's trying to dispel), the truth is that he's brought a vulnerability and sensitivity to Sonny Crockett that's far above and beyond anything else seen on prime-time TV. For confirmation, just tune in to *The A-Team* or *Airwolf* some evening.

While the ratings still weren't anything to celebrate, the demographics offered consolation: *Miami Vice* was picking up the teens and the women; they didn't expect to get the older audiences, knowing these were the folks for whom *Falcon Crest* had been created. These demographics did lead to a poor decision for the show's second season. Deciding to go after the teenage audience on *Vice*'s lead-in show, NBC came up with *Misfits of Science,* enough to make any halfway intelligent adolescent head for the computer games, or even the bedroom and schoolbooks.

Calling *Miami Vice* "a cousin" to MTV, Michael Mann was concentrating from the start on getting the right music and mixing it up with the action in just the right way. He encouraged the show's directors to come up with new and creative ways to use music, such as director Thomas Carter's concept in the opening episode, where he wanted "not to use music as just background but as psychological subtext, if you will."

Those who recall that episode will remember that Crockett's marriage had just broken up and that he'd just learned his ex-partner was leaking information to drug kingpins. Carter decided he'd like to do a scene with Tubbs and Crockett driving somewhere, with music laid over the video. What he came up with is what Carter told *Time* magazine "is probably the prototypical *Miami Vice* sequence."

In it, Crockett and Tubbs drive to an assignation, with Crockett stopping to make a call from a pay phone to his wife. As Crockett's sleek black Ferrari Daytona slides through the deserted nighttime streets of Miami, reflections shining off the polished fenders and wire wheels, Phil Collins sings his mournful ballad, "In the Air Tonight." When Crockett pulls up to a phone booth, the viewer almost gasps at the beauty of the video and audio coming together. The effect isn't unlike stepping into an Edward Hopper painting.

Miami Vice could afford to do things just like that, just as they could afford to spend in excess of $10,000 per episode buying the rights to the original recordings. That kind of money bought them familiar names and voices: Cyndi Lauper, Collins, Tina Turner, the Rolling Stones, Rockwell, the Coasters, Todd Rundgren, Power Station, U2, and Frankie Goes to Hollywood.

Musically, no expense was barred. Nor was any truly innovative idea naysaid. In the episode entitled "Smuggler's Blues," Glenn Frey's song of the same name was the basis for the whole plot, and the tune was played in snatches throughout the show's sixty minutes, setting the pace and the tone of the tale, making dialogue unnecessary for long stretches when the song itself outlined the action.

The success of *Miami Vice*'s musical counterpoint is the result of the efforts of two men. Associate producer and music coordinator Fred Lyle chooses the current hits for each show, while jazz virtuoso Jan Hammer composes and arranges an original score for the program.

Hammer was a founding member of the Mahavishnu Orchestra and has worked with artists like Jeff Beck, Al DiMeola, and Sarah Vaughan. He does most of his work for *Miami Vice* from his 150-year-old Colonial house outside Brewster, New York, where his studio holds an impressive array of state-of-the-art electronic gear.

Michael Mann gave Hammer carte blanche musically after Hammer came up with *Mi-*

ami Vice's intricate and recognizable theme music. Hammer is allowed to do all the work on his own, from the time a rough cut of the episode is delivered to his door by messenger until he sends his finished score back to the production company. It's an unusual arrangement, and one that suits the composer to a T. "The old style," as he told *Time* magazine, "was for the composer to sit in production meetings, and someone would say, 'Let's put something here,' or 'Let's put something there.' We have managed to bypass all that. The only occasional talk with Michael is when he wants even more music."

To get the "authentic" Calypso and reggae sounds that so subtly accompany and underscore the visuals and plots of the show, Hammer makes use of a Moog analog synthesizer, a Steinway, a guitar, and a Fairlight CMI digital player. With his battery of high-priced gadgets, Hammer can turn out anything from steel-band music to a string quartet. All it takes is the right hardware—and an incredible amount of skill. As Fred Lyle told *Rolling Stone*, "He's no three-chord rock-and-roller. One of the best things about my job is getting to talk to Jan Hammer."

As the word of mouth started circulating through the country, the ratings of *Miami Vice* started their slow climb to the top. The situation might have caused panic on any other network, but these folks were working for NBC, Grant Tinker and Brandon Tartikoff's NBC, so they knew the network would stick with them to justify these men's belief in the show.

And, as young audiences started tuning in and turning on to *Vice,* the series was definitely picking up audiences. NBC spokesman Brian Robinette was pleased when he could announce—in the spring of '85—that the ratings were showing a definite improvement, winning out over *Matt Houston* most weeks and even outdoing *Falcon Crest* some weeks. "The young women watching our show like the guys," Robinette said, "because they're manly and good-looking. And the men like them because they're traditional heroes."

Steadily, *Miami Vice* started showing its impact on the American consciousness. None of the production staff was surprised by the series' relentless climb to popularity, but some others were, including media analysts at *Vice*'s advertising agency in New York, Dancer, Fitzgerald and Sample. Mel Connor, one of the directors of network advertising with the agency, admitted in the spring, "We did underestimate its impact. It's a cult show with a lot of young people who like to watch it. We always thought it was arty and different, but with their use of colors, photography, and rock music—and the authentic Miami flavor it delivers—the young audience loves it. It's a high-style show. And it's exceptionally well directed."

It was also attracting the audience that had the most money to spend, which meant prospective advertisers were lining up and fighting to place their commercials into the program breaks.

By midway through that first season, it wasn't at all surprising to hear some hip young guy explaining he couldn't make plans for Friday night because he didn't want to miss the latest episode, or to see folks buying VCRs simply to record *Miami Vice* and be able to call Friday nights their own again.

The network was blasé about the ratings, knowing *Vice* was going to pick up plenty of ratings points when summer rolled around and *Matt Houston* and *Falcon Crest* went into reruns. And they were right. That summer *Miami Vice* shot up to a number-one position several times.

With its Necco wafer colors, its sun and sand motif, its tropical wardrobes, *Miami Vice* was the perfect summer show. It wasn't long before *Miami Vice* was setting the style for a fashion wave that was sweeping the country.

The "clothes-and-robbers" series used apparel to set the mood and carry through on the tertiary-color schemes from the first episode, and it wasn't long before everybody in America knew what the *Miami Vice* look was. And everyone wanted it. A "Berry's World" cartoon summed up the style fever when it depicted a male shopper trying on a white linen suit as a salesman fawned and said, "It's very *Miami Vice*-y." Suddenly, style and color were more important in men's fashions than ever before.

As with everything else on the program, nothing was left to chance in the wardrobe department. Costume designer Bambi Breakstone, in between her many trips to Paris, Milan, and London to choose outfits, explained, "The concept of the show is to be on top of all the latest fashion trends in Europe." Again, the style, the originality didn't come cheap, with $100,000 shopping sprees to dress Crockett and Tubbs in the newest thing from Gianni Versace, Hugo Boss, Vittorio Ricci.

The whole look was created by costume designer Jodi Tillen, who was thrilled when it caught on. The exact look wasn't available— or, as a rule, affordable—for most viewers because the clothes hadn't yet arrived on these shores when first shown on *Vice*. But money didn't have all that much to do with the look, according to Tillen, and men with a sense of style and an eye for Easter egg colors were putting together *Vice*-like wardrobes on their own. "Any man can fake it," Tillen advised. "All he has to do is take chances with style and, even more importantly, with color."

Viewers were bombarded with *Vice*'s particular fashion statement as Crockett and Tubbs managed five to eight wardrobe changes per episode. They always wore the approved colors—green, blue, pink, fuchsia, peach. And no earth tones.

"The show has made it OK for men to enjoy fashion and to wear color," Tillen said happily. "They're not threatened by it anymore. It doesn't mean you're less of a man if you wear lavender. It's just a shade. You don't have to be stuck with a gray suit and a white shirt.

"In fact, interesting color can be worn day or night, anywhere. And even more instructive, I think, men are learning from the show that they needn't worry about putting colors together *right*. There is no right or wrong. We present such eclectic use of color on the show that they realize they can't make a mistake, even if they're colorblind. They see Crockett, for example, in a lavender jacket with a baby-blue or peach T-shirt, and they like the look. . . ."

Tillen might have added it helps to be able to put oneself in the middle of the right scenery when so attired. When a guy's wearing a lavender jacket, it helps to have a peach wall to slouch against.

Don Johnson was the man who got to cash in on the fashion look in a major way, since Crockett's wardrobe was more accessible to young Americans than his partner's. Tubbs was conceptualized as having an urbane, New York look, one that called for double-breasted jackets with peaked lapels, dark shirts, angles, bright ties. Crockett's look was defined by Michael Mann as "casual chic." That meant single-breasted jackets with soft shapes and soft fabrics. And Crockett's look required only one legitimately expensive item—the linen jacket. As long as the jacket was authentic, the look could be finished off on a shoestring, with white espadrilles (canvas were acceptable, though Crockett's were leather), white duck or khaki pants with Italian front pleating, and pastel T-shirts. Any guy watching at home could acquire an entire wardrobe of T-shirts by doing just what *Vice*'s wardrobe department did: buying inexpensive undershirts and dying them various pastel hues.

With his gruff voice and five o'clock shadow, Don Johnson's Sonny Crockett was just the fellow to make wearing mauve macho. As *USA Today* put it, "In the era of the wimp, he packs a wallop."

And Don himself said, in tones no one would argue with, "It's the man who makes the clothes. It's how you wear the pink pants. It's not the pink pants. I wear damned well what I please."

Johnson, playing the "linen lion" on the television screen, found the look easy to carry over into real life. After all, what man wants to wear a tie and socks in hot weather if he doesn't have to?

While the rest of the world might consider the perquisite of a gorgeous, extravagant wardrobe in itself a great reward, Don's not all that impressed. "I can keep all of the wardrobe I want," he told *Playboy*. "But although the audience sees it for only five or ten minutes at a time, I sometimes have to wear it for days or weeks. So by the time the show is over, the outfit is dead to me, even though the actual fashion hasn't hit the streets. In fact, I wore a variation of my *Miami Vice* clothing long before I did the show. I figured a T-shirt, jeans, and a sports coat were right for anything short of meeting the queen."

114

Much more interesting to Johnson than the wardrobe were the type of people he was getting to meet. A longtime *Mod Squad* fan, he now found himself hanging out with real undercover detectives and drinking in the atmosphere. "You have to act very cool when you hang out with undercover cops because they're in pressure situations all the time," he said, not trying to hide the fact he was impressed. "They put their lives on the line every single minute they are out on the streets."

Recently, talking about the various undercover cops with whom he'd conversed, Don picked out the DEA agent who arrested auto manufacturer John DeLorean as one of the most interesting he'd met. He regaled Don with stories about his work and Don "would eat that stuff up. He described the adrenaline rush before a bust and what it was like to live undercover for weeks and to party with a guy and get close to him and know the whole time that you were going to nail him to the wall. The undercover cop is also acting—only it's the big acting in the sky. If you f— up, you don't get a bad review; you get shot."

By fall of 1985, there wasn't any doubt left in anyone's mind that *Miami Vice* was established and was going to be hanging in there for some time to come. Other folks were getting just as enthusiastic as Miamians, where the show had been number one in the local ratings since its debut. A study done by Marketing Evaluations/TvQ and reported in *TV Guide* testified to its success. When 1500 people were asked to name their favorite show of all those broadcast from March to August, the top three were *The Cosby Show, Miami Vice,* and *Highway to Heaven*.

And by September of 1985, Florida Hotel and Motel Association president Pedro Mandoki was crediting *Miami Vice* for the jump in tourism in the state, with July's occupancy up more than four points over the year before in Miami Beach, up nearly 13 percent in downtown Miami, and up almost 9 percent in the area surrounding Miami International Airport. Anyone left in Miami who wasn't already a *Vice* fan had to be converted by those figures.

Fifteen years after hitting Hollywood determined to leave the heartland behind, Don Johnson had arrived. He was a star. Paradoxically enough, he'd just had to leave Hollywood behind to get there.

9

TV's Sexiest Man

"They tell me that nothing like this has ever happened in TV. I mean, I walk into places and people look thunderstruck. It's all very perplexing, you know?"

That was Don Johnson's comment as *Miami Vice* swung into its second television season. And Don Johnson's second season in the sun. From being a has-been, he'd flashed like a shooting star into idolhood. For Don, it was a drastic change, to say the least. As Sonny Crockett, he'd become an even bigger star than any of those M-G-M executives had promised when he was the fresh-faced, wide-eyed Stanley Sweetheart.

The 1985–86 season started with NBC high in the ratings, and with all the network personnel thrilled with how *Miami Vice* had lived up to their expectations. More than lived up to them. It was time for the "Vicing" of America: a *"Miami Vice* Men's Department" opened in Macy's, and a *"Miami Vice* Collection" sprang from After Five, the *Miami Vice* glossy wall calendar hung on display in B. Dalton and Waldenbooks, the *Miami Vice* sound track album was ready for release, and the *Miami Vice* stars' every word and gesture was reported for voracious fans to read.

Don Johnson was the man the fans just couldn't get enough of. Every show wanted him as a guest—from David Letterman to *Entertainment Tonight*. No fact about him was too small to be interesting. His favorite ice cream is Haagen-Daz vanilla swiss almond? Let's run out and buy some. He likes the colors cobalt blue and gray? Let's redo the living room. He doesn't drink? Waiter, bring us some San Pellegrino. And if we can't get enough of *Miami Vice* on the TV screen, we can always buy the novelizations of our favorite episode. Of course, we've already traded in the old VCR for one with stereo since *Miami Vice* is a stereo broadcast. We don't have to shell out over eight

118

thousand bucks for a gold Rolex like Sonny Crockett's since Sonny's is a fake. Still, Don Johnson wears a Rolex in stainless steel, which isn't exactly cheap to come by.

With the fame came the rumors: Don Johnson was impossible to work with. Don Johnson was ditching his girlfriend. Don Johnson thought he was God.

Don's tried to field nasty rumors by announcing he's no more arrogant than he used to be, that he was *always* arrogant.

To a large degree, this is obviously true; his public persona hasn't changed much since the days back at Wichita South. Only, back then, nobody but Don's classmates knew who he was.

As for success going to his head, he hadn't yet become the biggest star in American television when he admitted to a reporter, "Sometimes, I'll start talking about something that I don't like, that isn't right, and Philip will say, 'You're getting ahead of the game.' It probably is unnerving for directors. But I want high standards. . . . I'm trying to learn better, though, how to express some of my criticism."

One person who has always backed up Don—perhaps as a result of that late-night talk they had back when they were shooting the pilot—is his costar. "Don has an exterior hardness," Philip Michael Johnson told *TV Guide*. "He wants everybody to believe he is a 'get the hell out of my way' type. Really *tough,* you know? Actually, he's a pretty spiritual, deep-thinking cat these days."

When he has time to think, that is. "It's a lot of work," Don has said wearily. "And sometimes it's so devastatingly difficult and there's so much pressure that I sit in [my] trailer and want to cry because I have to go out there and do it again."

More and more of Johnson seems to have crept into Crockett, and the role of Sonny hasn't suffered from it. And Don accepts Crockett, warts and all, which is more than some of his fans do with Johnson. "I like the character," he's said. "He's capable of making monumental mistakes. And he's capable of being selfish, impetuous, impulsive—and wrong. I get so sick and tired of seeing TV shows where the leads aren't capable of making mistakes. I think that portrays a false sense of what life is really all about."

Don Johnson and Sonny Crockett are so intermingled in viewers' minds by now that it's actually hard, if not impossible, to imagine another actor playing the role. As Don says, "It's very difficult to separate yourself from the character, especially a character who has the same sensibilities that I do. I think like Crockett. We share a very hard and tough exterior and a sarcastic wit that I think covers up a very idealistic and tender and gentle interior.

"Both Crockett and I love our work. He lives as an undercover cop. He loves that element of dealing with people. And I think people fascinate the hell out of him. I want him eventually to be running a social commentary with a sense of humor about everything he sees on the streets."

With the second season, some of the less popular aspects of the first season were dropped or underplayed. Crockett still lives on board his boat, the *St. Vitus Dance,* with his pet alligator Elvis, but neither is seen with the frequency of the past season. Meanwhile, Sonny's ex-wife has faded from the scripts other than the odd mention. And he no longer drops by to see his little boy—at least, not on the viewer's time. His romance with fellow cop Gina (Saundra Santiago) may never have happened except for an occasional meaningful look that passes between the two and reminds everyone she'd be happy to give him another chance if he'd just stop being such a womanizer.

From the very beginning, Don has spoken up when he thought something could be improved, just as he's kept his distance from the rest of the cast and the crew, ducking into his private RV whenever he's got a break. "I come in here and people on the crew probably think I'm rude," he said early in the series. "I won't have lunch with them. But it's just that I'm trying to sleep whenever I can."

In spite of the rumors, Don's never had anything but praise for his coworkers. "This is the most unselfish group of actors I've ever worked with," he told Emily Benedek. "We're a bunch of misfits, really. Every one of these people has paid his dues. The only thing that makes us feel good is to take these chances. We've been through drugs and alcohol and outlaws and thieves. The whole crew is reformed. I mean, we've been around the block. . . ."

If that sounds like something Sonny Crockett might have said, it's not surprising. When Johnson talks about the series, he often sounds more like a cop than an actor. "He watches my back and I watch his," is how he described his relationship with Thomas. "If a director comes in and puts Philip in a position that makes him look bad, I won't allow it to happen and vice versa. If another actor came in and tried to upstage one of us, he wouldn't last thirty seconds."

And he and Philip seem genuinely fond

and respectful of each other. "When you work as closely as we do and spend as much time together," according to Don, "you have to protect your relationship together and apart. So far, I've never worked with anyone I've had more fun with."

As for Johnson, Thomas says admiringly, "He's very well schooled in his craft. And he has a passion for perfection."

Blame that passion for perfection for some of the press reports claiming Don's temperamental and a pain to work with. "That's just press," he insists. "As an actor you have to be very selfish and maintain the integrity of your character while at the same time be unselfish as a person so you can create this unbroken chain of energy among the other actors, the director, the cameraman, and everybody else. It's a delicate balance. I know the show. I also know that I'm not going to let somebody come in and f— it up. So I try to be as diplomatic as possible, and I think I achieve that most of the time. I'm not difficult. I'm just demanding, but no more so on anybody else than I am on myself. Sometimes my perfectionism and my enthusiasm to get it as good as can possibly be is misconstrued as temperamental. But I do not throw tantrums or stomp off or yell at people. I have very enthusiastic creative discussions."

By the end of the first season, both Don and Philip agreed that the big problem in the future was going to be the writing. Don described the "biggest pain of our existence" as "scripts, trying to get a good one," while Philip admitted, "Some of the scripts have been turkeys."

Both actors have fought for the same trend, one which was noticeably more prevalent in the second season than in the first, and that's a more emotional psychological bent. Not necessarily less action, just more emotional truth.

In the meantime, there are the usual problems that come with any TV series, including an occasional director with whom neither actor is happy. Of one, Thomas remarked, "I told Don we were going to have to direct this one ourselves. It's not a matter of conceit. We have the responsibility of making him [the director] look good so he won't make us look bad." Not surprisingly, Don directed one of the second season's episodes himself, and gave Patti a role.

In spite of some of the drawbacks of the fame, Don likes it just fine. He's complained that "I will now go through life with those charming little cheap Japanese instant cameras stuck in my face the whole time. There are times when I want to take all the money

I make and buy all those cameras and throw them into the East River." But for the most part, he's thrilled to be exactly where he is.

"You work hard for years to achieve a certain amount of notoriety," Don said at the end of the first season. "I don't think any of us was prepared for the kind of success this was going to bring. . . . I have a theory. Most people get used to failure, because so much of the time you strive to accomplish something and it falls short of the mark. So you learn how to deal with failure a lot better than success. But after fifteen years of suffering and rejection, I'm enjoying success. It makes life so much sweeter."

Don's relatives were happy for his success, even though in the case of Don's father Wayne, it meant seeing his son less than in the past few years when Don and Patti were able to visit his farm in Wheelerville, Missouri, three or four times a year. "Understandably, my family is very excited about the show," Don told Nina L. Diamond. "They are so proud of me they're about to burst!"

In the wake of fame came fan mail, thousands upon thousands of letters, many from women who included pictures (many "X" rated) and phone numbers and said they'd like to come to Miami and spend some time with Don—doing anything his heart desired.

With fame came fortune, as well. And that part of success was no cause for complaints, though Don couldn't help feeling embarrassed when someone bid $5500 at a charity auction for a T-shirt on which he'd wiped his brow.

"There's a lot more to me than a guy in a three-dollar T-shirt and Versace jacket," Don's said, adding frankly, "though that part is very difficult to nurture these days. I like who I am. I miss myself."

He hasn't been missing out on all the pleasures money can buy, like a forty-foot motor home complete with full kitchen, wall-to-wall bed, and VCR, or a $125,000 customized, twin four-hundred-horsepower Scarab motorboat aptly yclept *My Vice*. He's also got the requisite bodyguard, a 6'1", 240-pound hulk named Ron Russell.

Like most stars who have big bucks coming in from a weekly series, Don's started to invest in real estate. He's bought houses in Los Angeles and Miami and is currently looking at places in New York City, a spot he seems more and more drawn to since his success.

One thing Don hasn't acquired with fame is the kind of vanity that leads actors to the plastic surgeon's office. On the show, Don wears little makeup, just a bit of touching up of the lines around his eyes, and in spite of a perpetual tan (a by-product of shooting in Miami), his looks are weathered, a map of all those long roads he's been down. "A lot of my friends are getting tucks and pinches and pulls," he told one reporter. "I can't imagine that. I have lived my whole life waiting for character lines." Don's world-weary looks are actually a great improvement upon his looks at twenty. Now there's character in his face, an almost lean and cunning look, a shadow of hurt around the eyes that stands in pleasing contrast to the baby-faced blond who starred in *The Magic Garden of Stanley Sweetheart*. It took him a long time to stop looking like a boy; now that he looks like a man, he has no desire to turn back the clock.

He's made stubble sexy, but the look isn't all that easy to achieve. Don's got to shave just like every other guy to maintain his Sonny Crockett two-day stubble. He just does his shaving with a sideburn trimmer instead of a safety razor.

Even with a hit series under his belt, Don doesn't feel he can let up for an instant, and this may be what some interpret as "attitude." No one who knows Don's story could blame him for wanting every detail exactly right. After all, he knows better than most actors how fleeting fame can be, especially when it comes to television. He's young enough to remember what happened to him back in 1970 and old enough to remember actors like Ed ("Kookie") Byrnes, Gardner McKay, Van Williams, George Maharis, MacLean Stevenson.

"I think about that a lot," he confessed recently when discussing the thin line separating today's hot star from tomorrow's used-to-be. "What strikes me about fame is that once you achieve it, there's nothing left to become but infamous. And if you make a few wrong decisions, infamy is what you end up with. Maybe that's why I'm always on edge."

It looks as if Don Johnson's here to stay this time around. And NBC, the network that almost passed him by, is more than happy to do what it can to accommodate him, knowing Don's played a big part in its ratings revival. The opening *Miami Vice* episode of the 1985 fall season placed eighth in the A. C. Nielsen Company ratings, helping to make it truly an "Amazing Week" for NBC. And the week *The Long Hot Summer* screened the first of two parts, with Don in the Paul Newman role, NBC had another ratings victory, with *The Long Hot Summer* ranking seventh and *Miami Vice,* in sixteenth place, beating out an original episode of *Falcon Crest* for the first time ever.

The talk started during the 1985 season that Don might not be long for the show since other offers were starting to come his way. The actor was frank about his desire to direct—and to direct more than *Miami Vice* episodes. His goal is to make movies and he likes to have control; naturally, his interest would be in directing. Eventually, he'd like to have his own company "and to be able to make movies with the best people I can find."

As for *Miami Vice,* Don thinks it's going to be around for a long time, with or without him, saying, "As long as there are drug smuggling and rock-and-roll, it will stay on the air."

How long will Don stick with the show? That depends. He's said from the very start that the moment it becomes boring, he'll leave. He can't predict when that might be.

Don says when he looks at himself in the mirror every morning, he's proud, proud of his success and proud of the fact that he hung in there when it looked as if he wasn't going to make it. He says he "clawed" his way to the top and deserves to be there, and in moments of glee, he's been known to shout half jokingly, "Everybody loves me, everybody wants me!"

At thirty-six, he gloats that he still doesn't know how to tie a tie. He doesn't have to know, anyway, so he's free to direct the energy he once spent partying into pursuing a multifaceted future. "I want to act and I want to direct and I want to produce and I want to sing and dance," he said not long ago. "I want to do it all." He left out any writing ambitions, but it's a safe bet he's got those, since way back in the *Stanley Sweetheart* days he was already trying his hand at a screenplay, which he described at the time as being about two ordinary people who "just happen to be lovers and just happen to be killers." Not exactly your ordinary couple, but then, Don Johnson was never exactly your ordinary guy.

Right now, Don's enjoying basking in the limelight and in the stardom he waited so long to achieve. And he's got the satisfaction of knowing his series is an inspiration to other actors, directors, and writers and is helping to shape the future of television. As director Bobby Roth said, "The old stigma against TV is now gone. A lot of shows are going to sound better, and they are going to look better. And I think *Miami Vice* is a big reason for that." Roth is seconded by *St. Elsewhere* cocreator Joshua Brand, who, after signing on to coproduce Steven Spielberg's *Amazing Stories*, said *Miami Vice*'s success "shows that people *do* notice production values, lighting, and what comes out of those little television speakers."

Of course, not everyone admits to being all that impressed with TV's hottest series. Some, like *St. Elsewhere*'s executive producer Bruce Paltrow, dismiss the show as just another cop show, glib rather than deep.

But the Bruce Paltrows of this world are, right now, in the minority. The majority, fans and television people alike, agree with Philip Michael Thomas that *Miami Vice* is unique, a phenomenon, and that the folks making the series are not just making hackneyed television fare but "making gold."

10

The Not
So Mod Squad

What about the other talented actors on *Miami Vice*? Don't they feel left out with Johnson getting almost all the attention? Many of the supporting cast members have made public criticisms, but they're critical of the show—and their roles on it—and never of Don.

John Diehl, who plays Zito, and Michael Talbott, his partner Switek, would both be happy if their characters were used more often and were a bit better-rounded. Of Zito, Diehl has said, "I want to get away from depicting him like a buffoon ... just comic relief. I heard it was never conceived as an ensemble piece. But if they want to do *Starsky and Hutch,* all right."

And Michael Talbott has said bluntly, "First there's Michael Mann, then there's Miami, then there's the look, then there's the music, then there's Don and Philip, then there's the alligator. We're way down on the list."

Though it's understandable that they'd like their characters to have some of the psychological and emotional nuances Johnson and Thomas are going after, the truth is that these guys are great. Yes, they *should* be given more to do, because no matter how small their roles are in any particular episode, they shine. Richard T. Jameson in *Business Week* echoed the sentiments of many viewers when he confessed that Switek and Zito "have started to grow on me. The actors' behavioralism saves us, persuading us of the abiding serenity with which these two utter goombahs assume that they, too, have a place in the order of things. That Diehl happens to resemble John Sayles with brain damage only adds to the esoteric charm."

Switek and Zito supply just about all the comic relief the show gets on a regular basis (guest stars like Charlie Barnett often supply their own share), and viewers have come to love the two Hawaiian-shirted undercover cops who often pose as exterminators.

In fact, one of the best *Miami Vice* episodes of the first season was the one that focused on Switek and Zito. Who'll ever forget Zito's house burning down, forcing him to move in with his partner, who just happened to be living with Zito's ex-girlfriend Darlene? And who'll forget Zito's soliloquy to his goldfish or Switek's enraptured praise of Elvis Presley? Buffoons? No way. Diehl and Talbott come across as two skilled performers who bring depth and humanity to their roles.

The women's roles have gotten more complex and less stereotyped since the beginning episodes, good news for those who admire the acting talents—and not just the physical attributes—of Saundra Santiago and Olivia Brown. As Gina Calabrese and Trudy Joplin, they've been given more to do than just coddle the men and hit the street as undercover hookers. *Miami Vice* has come a long way since Santiago complained, "I don't think they know what to do with women; it's such a man's show. I keep telling Michael Mann, 'I want to work. You're paying me all this money, please use me.'" Still, it's got a way to go. Women—with the exception of Pam Grier, who was terrific in her two appearances as Valerie, the only woman *Vice* has shown Tubbs falling for, and whose character was strongly developed and fully realized—are usually sex objects or *just* objects, manipulated around to fill out a scene or to take up space. Or, occasionally, as in Sylvia Miles's memorable cameo as Mrs. Goldberg, they provide a laugh or two. It's a tribute to Miles that she could play yet another variation of a role she's played so many times before and still make it hysterically funny.

Brown, who'd done little before *Miami Vice* other than playing the girl Eddie Murphy met in a bar in *48 HRS,* seems to have no complaints. Her husband, fellow actor Mykel T. Williamson, has appeared as a *Miami Vice* guest star.

The man who acts happy as a clam about his role on the series is probably the most serious artist of the lot. But Edward James Olmos hasn't a bad word to say about playing Lieutenant Castillo. The role has given him more exposure than ever before in his career—and a Best Supporting Actor Emmy, to boot. "Maybe it shocked the other cast members that they were going to be in the position they're in," he said shortly after joining the show. "I had no qualms. None."

So great is Olmos's power in the role of the stone-faced Castillo that it's easy to for-

135

get he wasn't one of the original cast members. Gregory Sierra was Crockett and Tubb's boss in the first couple of episodes, and his role was decidedly bland, certainly a waste of a talented actor. But Castillo, though expressionless, is hardly bland at all. He's the original mystery man, with a melancholy exterior and a past that's often hinted at but never fully explained. He's also a favorite with female viewers—that craggy, pockmarked visage seems to mask incredible sensuality and passion.

Off screen, Olmos is a passionate and committed actor, born in Los Angeles but ever mindful of his Mexican heritage. In 1979 he won a Tony nomination for his electrifying supporting role in *Zoot Suit*. Four years later he produced and starred in the critically acclaimed film, *The Ballad of Gregorio Cortez*.

Though no brooding Castillo in real life (people are always suprised to find out how friendly he is), Olmos does have an innate seriousness, and he approaches the role of the unsmiling lieutenant with concentration and dedication, describing his alter ego as "a Ninja warrior." The producers knew a great actor when they saw one; they gave him an unusual contract which allows him to do other work during the season as well as the go-ahead to play Castillo the way he wanted. In doing so, they let the man create one of the most unforgettable characters on television, a portrayal for which the Academy of Television Arts and Sciences honored him. He began his acceptance speech by remarking that Castillo does indeed smile at times; he was so overjoyed at this recognition of his talent after many years as an actor that it's doubtful he could have repressed that triumphant grin no matter how hard he concentrated.

Don Johnson has praised the man who walked away with an Emmy the night Johnson didn't, saying, "Eddie Olmos has the character down so well that he doesn't even have to talk anymore. All he has to do is *look*."

And as far as the Emmy itself is concerned, Don, who lost out to *St. Elsewhere*'s William Daniels, was a good sport about not getting that statuette. "I was disappointed for the show," he admitted afterward. "I never expected myself to be nominated—which I thought was wonderful—and never expected to win. But what surprised me was that we didn't win for some of the obvious categories: the costumes, the music—Jan Hammer—the show itself. The awards are supposed to be for outstanding achievement, and I don't think there was any other show that achieved more outstandingly than our show this year. . . ."

As for Philip Michael Thomas, he has yet to betray any jealousy or resentment toward his costar. Of course, Philip, who's given to hyperbole and words like "phenomenal" and "incredible" and could outdo Mohammed Ali at "I am the greatest," always manages to turn any talk of Don around to . . . guess who?

"I'm so happy for Don. Are you kidding?" he said when asked if he envied Johnson's superstar status. "I get the same attention. If you were with us anywhere, you would see it as an equal relationship. There's no need for jealousy. Besides, I've been getting this kind of attention all my life. It didn't just happen because of *Miami Vice,* but a lot of America is just being introduced to Philip Michael Thomas."

"Philip's just visiting," Don once said, laughing, when asked about his partner. "I kid all the time about it. He's out there, man. He's dealing on a whole different level, but I love him like a brother. He can do whatever he wants and I'll swear and be damned by it. I'll support him to the ends of the earth. Now, in all honesty, some of the things he says catch me offguard to where I've stopped and said, 'Gee, that's a new concept, Philip.' But he's my partner. I'm very protective of everyone on the show, because nobody realizes the stress, strife, and turmoil we have to go through daily. We work at least twelve to fourteen hours a day, five days a week."

Fourteen hours a day with Philip Michael Thomas must be quite an education, because the guy's incredibly entertaining to listen to. And as Don said, some of the things that pop out of Thomas's mouth are truly, um, "out there."

For instance, he explains that TV is "neurolinguistic programming, or hypnosis" and leaves a permanent image in the brain. Of himself and Johnson, he says "I knew we were a bomb waiting to explode. We had the talent, technology, and timing." He says, "I'm a very serious businessman. I think of myself as an ultrapreneur. Ultra meaning the highest."

Producer John Nicolella echoed Don's appraisal of Thomas, telling *USA Today* reporter Monica Collins, "Philip will say a lot of strange things. But he's a kid at heart."

On the subject of his hit series, Philip "the kid" once boasted, "Without me, *Miami Vice* would not exist. I'm aware of that. I bring the magic. There's a kind of thing that Don and I create. Bring any other actor in and you won't see that."

Philip has another explanation for his success: "I am on such a strong power. I just turned thirty-six, which is a nine—three plus six is nine—and after this year, it's like ones and eights, power, power, power, all the way." (He seems to have forgotten that thirty-eight is a two, thirty-nine is a three, forty is a four, forty-one is a five, and so on.)

Thomas does have a complaint about the series, and it's one he thinks has a lot to do with Johnson's winning the glory and the Emmy nomination. And his point of criticism is well taken when he notes, "You know that Don's character is much more defined than my character. I mean, where does Tubbs live? What kind of a car does he drive? Does he have a mother and a father? Does he have a past, present, and future? No one knows." Tubbs, if viewers recall, was introduced in the premiere episode as an ex–New York City police officer who came down to Miami looking for Calderone, his brother's killer. But little personal information about the character has been introduced since then.

Philip's been quoted as saying he plans to leave the show in 1987 and that he sees *Miami Vice* as simply a stepping-stone in his journey of success. He's already started diversifying his career interests. He's into real estate holdings and is busy renovating a theater in Miami. Perhaps he'll stage *The Legend of Stagger Lee,* to which he's bought the rights, there. While he was out shopping around for properties, he also bought the film rights to the Pulitzer Prize–winning show, *No Place to Be Somebody.*

He's a self-defined workaholic, perhaps a result of his Seventh Day Adventist background. He even writes music on the set—between shots!

Last year, Thomas formed a partnership with a designer named Lhin Yi Bisogno to create three lines of women's sportswear sold under his name for their Miami-based company, Point Blank. The first collection featured about forty pieces, all in natural fabrics, with prices ranging from $30 to $120. The clothes, featuring fashion details like staggered hems, scooped-out side, and a skirt that turns into a sundress, use lots of floral prints. Very *Miami Vice*-y.

Much of his time since he signed on to star in *Vice* has been devoted to recording and promoting his album, *Living the Book of My Life,* produced by his own company, P.M.T., which just happens to stand for Perfect Moment of Truth, not a surprising corporate identity for a man who made his stage debut in *Hair.* Philip, who says he's "*seriously* into music," not only composed and coproduced the songs on his album, he also sang, played guitar and keyboards, and spoke of releasing the LP on his own label, Space Ship Records. Whew! His modest aim? How about becoming the number-one male recording artist in the world?

If self-confidence and doggedness are what it takes to become a billionaire, then Thomas, who's part American black, part American Indian, part Irish and part German ("Gumbo," he says), should soon be making Howard Hughes turn over in his grave. He's already spent more than $100,000 producing his album, but he's not worrying, because, as he said last year, "It's nice to be in this place—part of the winning team. You can parlay your talents from this place, and I intend to parlay them right to the top. I didn't get into this business to make $1.86. I got in to make it big. It's so nice being at the top!"

Is Thomas's ego really as big as he makes out? Or is his tongue firmly wedged in cheek? It's likely Thomas has cleverly fashioned his amusing brand of braggadocio to keep the reporters entertained and away from his private life, because this is a man who's basically secretive. He'll go on and on about how great he is, sure. And he loves talking about his family, especially his mother, who went back to school after her children were grown and got her B.A.; his brother (and bodyguard) George; his older brother and former star athlete Marcus; and his aunt, Elouise McMorris, who was the first black woman ever to receive a Ph.D. in chemistry.

What he doesn't like talking about is the private life of Philip Michael Thomas: his ex-wife, now a law student; his twelve-year-old daughter; the father he didn't see for sixteen years; the woman or women in his life. No, he'd rather discuss his image: "Sensuality is one of my best assets, but I try to be a health symbol instead, inside and out." Or he's happy to talk about any of the subjects he reads up on constantly: philosophy, higher learning, law, spaceships, and the Bible.

Don Johnson elbowing out Philip Michael Thomas? One person who's not worrying is Rico Tubbs himself. At least for public consumption, his ego is impermeable. He even managed to explain to one reporter how Don's being up for an Emmy was a reflection on the terrific talent of none other than PMT himself!

Oh, yes, the clothing being manufactured

143

by Point Blank has three different labels: "Naturally, PMT," "Of course, PMT," and "Definitely, PMT." PMT doesn't seem to be worrying much about DWJ's success at all!

11

"Quick"-ening the Pace

Has success changed Don Johnson? Yes. And no.

Don himself says he's *had* to change since his status in this world changed, but as far as his personality, he insists he's the same as always. As he told Susan Shapiro, "People ask me if I've changed because of my success and I tell them, no, I was arrogant and an ass before I made it, and I'll still arrogant and an ass!

"Am I going to scream no more press? Live like a recluse? Become more demanding?" he went on. "Yes. All of those things! This may be the last interview I do. . . . Ev-

145

erything's been said and printed and copied and shuffled and resaid and reprinted about eight million dozen times and I'm bored with it myself. I don't want people to get bored with it. I've fulfilled my obligations to the Great Machine and now I'm going to go and do my work!"

Don's reluctance to talk to the press lately no doubt accounts for much of the bad rap he's getting. They say he's impossible to get to, which is understandable since, unless he gave up acting, the man just wouldn't physically have the time to do all the interviews he's asked to do. They say he's got a swollen head and will no longer do interviews with Philip Michael Thomas because he considers himself the real star of the show. This seems like no more than kvetching, since an interview with the two of them appeared in the November 1985 *Playboy*. Besides, why wouldn't Philip Michael Thomas prefer doing interviews on his own as well? Philip has a *lot* to say, and when he's been interviewed by himself, he's had more of a chance to say it.

Don's situation is further complicated by the fact that he's got two public-relations firms handling him, firms that are sometimes at cross purposes. Rogers and Cowan, probably the biggest and most powerful entertainment PR firm in the game, handles *Miami Vice*'s publicity while PMK handles Don personally. Don's finding you just can't please all of the people all of the time, not if you want to have a few seconds left over to play with your son or just breathe.

He's reached the point where it's a rare occasion indeed when he gets through a meal in a restaurant (his favorite dish is pasta primavera al dente) without being disturbed by eager and sometimes obnoxious fans. "People basically want contact," he understands; still, he's hassled by the infringements on his privacy, by all those little cameras being stuck in his face. Right now he's still obligingly signing autographs for children, but when an adult comes along and shoves a piece of paper under his nose, he simply hands the fan a card that says: "Sorry you caught me at an inconvenient moment. Thank you for appreciating my work. If you would like an autographed picture, please write to: Don Johnson Fan Club, 2895 Biscayne Boulevard, Suite 395, Miami, Florida 33137." Those who send for a photo are likely to receive one signed, "Love and Kisses in all the right places," surely a salutation in keeping with exactly what most of his fans would like from him!

He says he does have a sizable ego but

that "it's in proportion. . . . Most people expect me to be more stuck on myself, more inaccessible than I am. . . ." And as far as humility's concerned, he says wryly, "I've been humbled by the best of 'em, believe me. I think the *most* humbling experience was my fifteen years in Hollywood. That's the most humbling experience *anybody* can have. . . ."

Johnson still remembers all those rejections he suffered along the way, and when he won the People's Choice Award, he wanted to make a speech saying, "I'm accepting this for all the actors that were too short, too fat, too pretty, too ugly, too big, too small, too good, too bad. Thank you."

Does the guy who's said he was pretty even as a child really think he's attractive? When he was asked that question by Nancy Collins, he answered, "Yeah, but not as attractive as a lot of people seem to think I am. To be picky, I have these hoods over my eyes that are not particularly attractive, and I have dirty dishwater-blond hair and dark eyebrows. Most people think I've bleached my hair or dyed my eyebrows, which annoys me because I'm a purist when it comes to that." Also, believe it or not, not everyone thinks Don Johnson's the best-looking thing in pink pants. He was once told his eyes were too close together!

A certain amount of vanity and self-regard go with the territory he's chosen. After all, looking good is part of his business. "I didn't used to think I was vain," he recently confessed. "I've since adjusted my opinion of myself. I am vain to the point that I like to feel good. I don't go to great pains, use a lot of creams and astringents, but I like to feel good and look good. Calisthenics, push-ups, and running, that is vanity, a well-placed vanity. So I guess I am vain, but I don't spend a lot of time [looking] in the mirror. Now I know people on the set ... will say that's bull, he's always looking in the mirror right before a take. But I don't look at my face, I look to see how the character is designed."

Don's happy and proud of himself, and who can blame him? After the first season, he and Philip saw their salaries jump from $20,000 an episode to $30,000 (and regardless of who may get the most publicity, they both get paid the same), with a raise up to $50,000 if the series runs two more years. Combined with the other money coming in, both actors should have reached millionaire status by the end of 1986. "I feel just right," Don says happily. "Life is good. It's a new high, knowing that I'll be working next year. You become an actor by being a shadow. I've been the shadow. Now I'll be the light."

And he is a brilliant light. In a report following the Live Aid concert in the summer of 1985, *Rolling Stone* reported that groupies were brushing past Mick Jagger just to get closer to Don! That's what making it is all about.

Don, who defines himself as "a maniac for details," has been reorganizing his business dealings so he can oversee almost everything himself. This, by the way, extends even down to the telephone—unlike many stars of his magnitude, Don returns most of his calls (except those from strangers, of course) himself. He has no manager, nor does he plan to hire one. Instead he relies on his agent and two attorneys for advice. The end decision, however, is all Don's. He wants things handled a certain way and doesn't expect anyone else, paid retainer or not, to care as much as he does how things turn out. He learned a long time ago just how little being surrounded by a bunch of people telling you you're the greatest star is actually worth when the time comes to cash in. And he knows what he's doing. According to John Nicolella, "If Don calls someone a boobhead, certainly I know where it's going and why. He doesn't want to accept mediocrity."

Don knows his perfectionism, and a ruthlessness that extends even to himself, are liabilities, and he does try to relax. But it's not easy for the man who admits he's pretty obsessive and that "people tell me to lighten up, but I don't know how."

Two things are helping him learn how: financial success and artistic freedom. Not long ago he admitted, "I'm different than I used to be. You know that Cyndi Lauper song, 'Money Changes Everything'? It's true."

Artistic freedom doesn't always come along with fame, but in Don's case, it has—so far, at least. He's a multitalented person and an actor capable of variety above and beyond the role of Sonny Crockett. And NBC, knowing a good thing when they saw one, encouraged Don to stretch his talent by starring in a TV movie, for their network.

Don picked up an extra $300,000 in 1985 for playing the role of Ben Quick in the two-part, four-hour movie, *The Long Hot Summer*, shown for two consecutive nights in October. He had some mighty impressive shoes to fill: in the 1958 big-screen version, Paul Newman had taken the part. This time around, Judith Ivey played Noel Varner (Joanne Woodward in the film) and Cybill Shepherd played Noel's hot-blooded sister-in-law Eula (portrayed by Lee Remick in '58).

The movie told the story of Ben Quick and the Varners and was based on William Faulkner's *The Hamlet* along with several other of his stories. Roughly, the story is concerned with wealthy old Will Varner, father of the shiftless Jody and the repressed Noel (in the film version, she was called "Clara," but that was undoubtedly not glamorous enough for television). When drifter and suspected barn-burner Quick turns up in town, old man Varner takes a liking to him, so much so that he starts grooming Quick to beat out son Jody in the family business and marry Noel.

The Long Hot Summer took two months of filming to make and ran over its budget, costing between $6 and $7 million. Its reviews and ratings ended up justifying the time and the expense.

Don arrived on location in Texas very much the star. At his own expense, he brought with him Mr. Jones, his golden retriever, his driver and cook, Sam Conigliaro and Sam's wife, his personal assistant Merry Williams, a portable sauna, and his new silver-gray 500 SEL Mercedes. If that sounds glamorous, consider this: the mosquitoes were biting like crazy, it was 104 degrees in the shade, and the cast and crew worked fourteen hours a day trying to get back on something resembling the original schedule.

A country boy all the way, as he's called

himself, Don could really sink his teeth into the role of Ben Quick, leaving many viewers surprised and impressed. Don Johnson wasn't *really* Sonny Crockett, after all. He was an actor who could make himself just as believable as the hot-blooded, smooth-talking drifter.

With torrid weather and a screwed-up shooting schedule, things weren't all sweetness and light in Marshall, Texas. "I've never been on a production where they had you sitting around waiting so much," Cybill Shepherd complained, adding that everyone was "uptight on this set." She'd read six books in two weeks by that time, while Ava Gardner was stuck there for four weeks with only six days of work.

Tension was the byword. When coproducer Len Hill arrived in town to check out the shooting slowdown, he noted worriedly, "There's not much camaraderie here."

And his coproducer John Lenox described the experience as *"tsoris,"* which is Yiddish for "trouble."

Was anybody happy? Certainly not the extras, some of whom were discovering their thirty-five-dollar-per-day fee had some extra "benefits" they'd have gladly done without—like heatstroke and sunburn.

For the most part, Don kept his cool, though

he lost it publicly at least once, when an assistant director called for quiet and someone neglected to turn off a truck's motor. According to *TV Guide,* a local, who watched as Don let loose with an expletive-studded venting of steam, said with a smile, "I wouldn't want to cross him. He's real demanding." Yep, that he is, and he'd be the first one to admit it, mister.

For the most part, the stars, including veteran actor Jason Robards, kept to their air-conditioned RVs, and Cybill Shepherd even paid to have her own trailer transported to the Lone Star State since it offered more comfort than the RVs provided by the production department.

For the most part, Johnson was enthusiastic about his role and as good a sport as possible about the adverse working conditions. The TV version, written by Rita Mae Brown, threw in some action the 1958 version lacked, adding a bit more violence and slapping around of Eula than Lee Remick received. Shepherd wasn't crazy about her character; in fact, offscreen, she'd do a quick impression of Eula shrilling, "Oh, *beat* me!"

Cybill's never had a reputation for being easygoing, but she and Don hit it off beautifully, maybe because in many ways, they're a lot alike. "She's irrepressible," Don said during the shooting. "I call her a brat. She is an actress with depth that's never been tapped. If anybody ever does tap that source, the sky's the limit. And she protects the integrity of the character she's playing."

Even after a wrap had been called, Don was still a Cybill fan, saying, "Cybill, Cybill, Cybill, she's the greatest. I could have a serious affair with Cybill. Most people don't get along with her. Not me . . ."

And though she did go on record as saying Jason Robards was absolutely the sexiest man on the set, Cybill later crossed her legs and started swinging the top one at the mention of Don's name by a *People* magazine reporter, saying sexily, "Look at me. Body language. It's a dead giveaway."

And Judith Ivey, who, as Noel, didn't get any lines as devastating as her wisecracks in *Compromising Positions,* said of working with Don, "If it ever gets boring, you've got somebody fabulous to look at."

Don was, as they say, very "into" his part. Just as he's always related Sonny Crockett to his own life, so did he build the character of Quick out of his own idiom, explaining, "He walks into the room, and a jar falls off the shelf. He causes things to happen because of his energy. He's a roadie right off a rock-and-roll band—well traveled, but he's

155

never gone first class." If Faulkner had still been alive, no doubt he'd have wondered what the hell Don was talking about.

As for Don's skills as an actor, he was praised by everyone. Director Stuart Cooper said admiringly, "It's been a long time since I've worked with an actor so camera-wise and intelligent. Don's like Newman and McQueen; he knows where the camera is and he puts his performance right into the lens." And John Lenox spoke of Don's having the same charisma Clark Gable possessed.

Don himself was characteristically modest about his performance, stating simply and lightly, "I'm not bumping into furniture." Far from it. He was almost unanimously lauded for his portrayal, which put him one step farther toward his goal of starring in another feature film.

Even before shooting *The Long Hot Summer,* Don had remarked with satisfaction, "I've had this angel on my shoulder, keeping me alive and keeping me together in spite of myself, in spite of a lot of things I did and places I've seen.

"For so many years . . . I kept saying to myself, 'Yeah, but when is it going to be my turn?' There are a lot of big stars in this business, guys that I kept being the bridesmaid to. Now, I'm being considered for the things targeted to them. I'm offered everything, from classics to the things ... targeted to Harrison Ford."

After *The Long Hot Summer,* Don gleefully revealed he was looking forward to making a feature during his next *Vice* hiatus. If he wanted to do something, he exclaimed, he'd just have to say so and six people would jump, with their checkbooks, and ask, "How much?" That's an enviable position for an actor, any actor, to be in. For Don, it's magical. There were all those years when those same six people would probably have said no more than, "Don Johnson? Well, who else is available?"

He's got other projects and possibilities on tap beside a starring role in a feature film. For one thing, there's the stage, of which he's said, "I want to go back to the theater someday. Roots, babe, you've gotta stay on top of things."

For another, there's his music. Don says he originally started writing songs "to occupy my creative energy." In addition to his work with Dicky Betts, he's done some cowriting with John Rubenstein. And he'll soon be releasing an album, on which he'll play guitar as well as sing.

Perhaps as practice for his upcoming musical career, Don's been likely to just pop up on stage as a guest when various groups are appearing in the Miami area. In March of 1985, he joined Prince on stage at the Orange Bowl (probably one of the few performers who makes the *Miami Vice* wardrobe look drab). Later, while shooting some scenes from *The Long Hot Summer* not in Texas but in New Orleans, Don hooked up with his pals Jimmy Buffett and Dan Fogelberg to see the Neville Brothers at a local jazz festival. Charmaine Neville handed Don a tambourine and he jumped right in on "Amazing Grace." And at Miami's Sportatorium, he sang "Some Guys Have All the Luck" and "Bang a Gong" on stage with Power Station. That group also appeared as a band in a club on *Miami Vice,* with band member John Taylor (also of Duran Duran) getting a small speaking part.

As *Miami Vice* winds down its second season, and Don Johnson's second season in the sun, Don's taking careful measure of the opportunities set before him. For perhaps the first time in his life, he's not rushing headlong into anything. He's sitting back and weighing each offer cautiously, taking care not to make the wrong decision, to do the wrong interview. It can be exhausting. "You fight to get to this position and then you fight to keep from being like a trained animal act," he said wearily after folks started referring to him as "the sexiest man on television."

Johnson doesn't have to read through scripts looking for three or four films to do a year. For one thing, he hasn't got the spare time to take on that much extra work. For another, he shies away from overexposure. With folks able to catch him weekly on *Miami Vice,* too many other appearances at this time could bring on a case of overkill. And the last thing Don wants to do is bore anyone since he so dislikes being bored himself.

For the time being he's still too much like a kid with a new toy to be bored, really and truly bored. His fellow *Miami Vice* cast members teased him last year when he got a satellite dish for his RV. "Why shouldn't I have one?" he asked sensibly. Why, indeed, shouldn't he have it all? There's no denying that after more than a decade of heavy dues paying, Don Johnson's earned it, in spades.

12

Father and Son

"It is very difficult for an actor who is away from his family while on location to maintain a good relationship," Don has said. Ever since the press started considering Don newsworthy instead of a nobody, rumors have flared that he and Patti D'Arbanville have split up. "It's all over," a gossip pundit will announce, and then, lo and behold, a few days later, Don will show up someplace with Patti by his side.

Of their living over two thousand miles apart, Don's jokingly said, "It's a helluva commute," but in spite of that, the two seem determined to stay together, regardless of what other people say.

Patti, who's last movie role was in *Real Genius,* knows her relationship with Don isn't exactly "conventional," but for the time being there's no alternative. She's as serious about her career as he is about his—she has been in the business almost as long as he has—and knows it would be all over for her as an actress if she moved to Florida. She knows how much momentum she lost in her career in this country by spending five years in Paris. And though it's literally closer, Miami is metaphorically just as far from Hollywood, especially for a woman who's looking to get her own television series.

For the time being, becoming Wife Number Four would appear to be out of the question. "We approach marriage like a viper in the grass," Don was quoted as saying in *Us* magazine, "as opposed to the way you should approach it, which is as a holy union in the eyes of God. We both had very bad experiences with marriages and we both come from broken homes. I think in our hearts and minds we're more married than any piece of paper you could ever sign. It's possible, but we have something very good happening which we don't want to screw up."

Don doesn't see any conflict between remaining unmarried and staying together. He's said, "I *have* made a commitment, but not in the traditional sense. I'm more committed—by my own self-inspired commitment, ungoverned by outside sources—than a lot of married people. As you can see, I'm still the little boy rebelling against authority. So, in a lot of ways things haven't changed. Maybe someday I will be mature or intelligent enough to adopt marriage into my mental view of our relationship. But Patti is very happy with things the way they are. Our feeling, since Jesse was born, is, if it's not broke, don't fix it."

If Don's not the world's biggest proponent of marriage, he's certainly a booster of fatherhood. He's got Jesse with him as often as possible, and it's not unusual to walk into Don's trailer wherever he's working and find the towheaded toddler sitting on Daddy's lap or playing with his toys.

"He's my pal," Don said proudly when Jesse visited him during the filming of *The Long Hot Summer*. "He comes out from California and gypsies around with Daddy. He's like me—he talks with his hands and loves pasta. On the set everyone falls in love with him. He loves to sing and dance, and he's got more energy than ten kids ought to have.

His mother and I did a hell of a job—and it was fun doing it."

Calling parenthood "the most poetic thing life has to offer," Don says he'd like to have more children, "a parcel" of them, and he says fatherhood put his life in perspective.

Though Jesse's obviously thriving on crossing the country to be able to spend a good deal of time with both Mommy and Daddy (he travels in the company of his nanny), it's hard on his folks. After Jesse spent one two-month period on location with his father, Don confessed that the separation "damned near killed Patti." But both have accepted the logistics of the situation. And as someone who grew up not seeing his father as often as he'd have liked, Don feels it's extremely important to spend as much time as he humanly can with Jesse, on one coast or the other.

Jesse is one of the main reasons Don isn't eager to return to Los Angeles on a full-time basis. "I love him to death," he told Nancy Collins reflectively. "He's my top priority, which is why I'm not going back to live permanently in Hollywood. I don't hate Hollywood in the sense of the industry at its pinnacle. What I hate is all the parasitical elements. That whole scene is so sordid and degenerate, and I don't want Jesse around

163

it. Life is an illusion at best, and then to
compound it with the distortions of Hollywood is like going from the frying pan into
the fire."

That's quite a mouthful from someone who
once bragged that the best things in Hollywood were free for a good-looking young man
who was available for partying at the drop
of a hat. But then, it's obviously his own
past he thinks of when he pictures Jesse
growing up in such a jaded, footloose atmosphere. Even someone who hadn't passed
through such painful Hollywood rites of pas-
sage would need to do no more than look at
the unhappy adolescences of many celebri-
ties' children to realize it's even harder than
usual to protect your children from the un-
derbelly of life when you live in the film
capital.

On the subject of monogamy, both he and
Patti say they took each other as lovers, not
as prisoners or hostages. When the question
of monogamy—never one of Don's strong
points, as he's apt to admit—comes up, Johnson more often than not sidesteps the question with remarks like, "Just because I have
the freedom does not mean I elect to take
that liberty."

Not that it's easy to mix a relationship
with being an idol to thousands upon thou-

sands of women, especially not for a man whose friends say it would be impossible to keep track of all the women he's had. Though he's said time and again that the last thing he's ever wanted to be is a sex symbol, Don isn't reticent when it comes to building up his sexy public image by casually dropping statements that paint him as an inveterate womanizer. "I really, really like women. I like everything about them. It's not blondes, not brunettes, not black hair. It's not long legs, short legs—it long *and* short legs. It's not big breasts or small breasts—it's big and small breasts. It's everything. . . ." That's not exactly the sort of quotation a woman sitting all the way on the other side of the United States wants to read as coming from the lips of the man she loves.

Don's described his sexual orientation as "sort of a desire to melt into women and then out of them. I can be satisfied just to be near a woman and smell her and touch her, to hold her hand, to watch her," he told *Playboy* interviewer David Rensin. "But this is very hard in a world that by and large sanctions monogamy. It's murder on relationships."

As his friends from Wichita all recall, flirting's always come naturally for Don. This is a guy who needs women, who basks in attention from the opposite sex, who's rarely been without at least one girlfriend. Maybe he never set out to be a sex symbol, but he can't help coming across as one. When he heard that he might be presenting the best actress award at the Emmy presentation (which, as it turned out, he was not asked to do), his immediate response was to quip, "I hope it's someone cute. I get to kiss 'em, you know." Lines like that come to his lips on their own accord.

Surprisingly, for a guy who's loved and left so many women, he managed to stay on good terms with quite a few of them. His old girlfriend Pamela Miller Des Barres is good friends not only with his ex-wife Melanie Griffith, but also with his current lady. And Patti and Melanie are friends, too. In Des Barres' eyes, "He's sort of *our* John Derek."

Though he says his commitment is to Patti, Don still talks of involvement with women in general in the present tense. "I've always had a reputation as a ladies' man," he informed Susan Shapiro. "But I've been discreet. I don't kiss and tell. If someone is attractive and throws three quick lines at me that get my attention, she's got me. If she makes me laugh, she's got me. I don't come on to women as a rule. I don't hand them lines. If I'm attracted to someone, I'll set the stage for an encounter, a dinner, an event. I'll manipulate the situation so that eventually we'll be together. I think women like the intrigue of that. It's very effective, more than the obvious one-liner." Sounds as if Don might have unconsciously spotted Patti *before* he decided to sit alone at the bar in Mr. Chow's, doesn't it?

Whether or not they live happily ever after or end up going their separate ways or make it legal and get married one of these days, the simple reality of the situation seems to be that in the here and now, Don and Patti care deeply about each other. Don termed it "pretty amazing to go through the things we've gone through in such a short time and still have a relationship that's growing, changing, redefining itself. It comes back to two people who care about each other tremendously."

He says Patti knows he'll always be there for the rest of her life "in the way we have defined-nondefined it," and that he'd never let anything happen to her or to Jesse. That certainly sounds like a commitment, contract or no.

And Patti's love and trust in Don are unbreakable. Talking to *People* magazine about the most thrilling night of both their lives, the evening they attended a state dinner at

167

the White House, Patti emotionally recalled, "Donny and I looked around and into each other's eyes and said, 'I love you.' We had come so far."

That appearance at the White House sparked off a great controversy—namely, did or didn't Don wear socks? Some reporters couldn't believe Sonny Crockett would bow to conformity, and spread the rumor. He did wear socks, black Christian Diors, to be exact. He even topped his tux off with a bow tie!

For a man who was wondering whether or not to pack up and move to Missouri to farm just a couple of years back, finding himself in the White House with the president and first lady was hard to believe. "It was the most enchanting evening I've ever spent in my life," he said afterward. "I mean, my God, the White House! I know there were a lot of people saying, 'What the f— is he doing at the White House?' And in fact, I said the same thing myself."

What he was doing was being a guest at a state dinner for the prime minister of Denmark. What he was *really* doing was being primed by Nancy Reagan to help her in her antidrug campaign.

"We were treated like royalty," Don said happily. "The president kept smiling and winking at Jesse. Right at the place they do the security check, Jesse kept looking at the Secret Service guys. When he saw one of their guns, he turned around and said loudly, 'Daddy, did you bring your gun?' I said, 'Shuuush, shuuush.' The Secret Service guys were getting nervous, but the president and first lady fell in love with him." Don sounded just like any proud daddy. But how many daddies are invited to chow down at the White House and requested to sign the president's copy of *Time* featuring *Miami Vice* on the cover afterward?

Don, older and wiser than he was when he first arrived on the Hollywood scene, is always agreeable to speaking out against drug use. He did an antidrug announcement during the summer of 1985 for WSBN, the National Broadcasting Company affiliate in Miami. Power Station's Michael Des Barres helped Don write the spot.

With original music playing in the background, Don spoke straight to his audience, telling them, "I'm talking to you. You use drugs. I've been where you are. Drugs don't work for me anymore. Don't let them ruin your life." The public-service commercial was entered for a local Emmy.

If anyone could "deglamorize" drugs, you'd think it would be rugged, worldly-wise Don

Johnson. But Don says people continue to approach him with cocaine or a joint, thinking they can get on close terms with the star by getting him high. He sets them straight in no uncertain terms, telling them that he doesn't do drugs—or hang around with people who do.

Still, it's not possible to change an image overnight. Then, too, some people don't pay attention, while others encourage folks to drink and do dope. Don's said exasperatedly that even after he'd spoken to the press about quitting drugs and alcohol and his problems with both, NBC and Universal continued to send him champagne to celebrate *Miami Vice*'s improved ratings. In the end, he was driven to send out a memo asking for baskets of fruit or chocolate if they really felt they had to send him something as a celebratory gesture.

Don's not fooling around when he says he's given up the fast lane for good. In fact, he continues to go to drug and alcohol treatment meetings, recognizing that alcoholism is a progressive disease. He doesn't have to wallow in booze and mind-benders anymore; he says he just wants to "get down and wallow" in life.

Though he insists he's had his heart broken by a lot of women that he got but couldn't keep (he'll rarely admit to not being able to get someone in the first place), Don's more the heartbreaker than heartbreakee type. He can't stop charming women of all ages, shapes and sizes, whether he's sending Jane Pauley a two-pound box of Godiva chocolates or Madonna flowers and a note signed, "With major lust. Don Johnson."

It's no wonder Don inspires the kind of adoration that turns usually cool, sophisticated females into worshipful fans who are willing to spend the whole night on the sidewalk just to see their idol shoot a scene in the street the following day. Speaking of romance, Don once said there are no victims and no accidents, only opportunities. Opportunities with Don Johnson are the sort most red-blooded women would give anything to have.

13

Having It All

Don Johnson sits in California or in Miami and he can say with confidence he's come a long way from the heartland, because now he knows he'll never have to go back there again, except by choice. He's emerged as *the* star of the mid-eighties, and his abilities have not yet been fully tapped. Like his friend Cybill Shepherd, he's got a lot of talent, only the surface of which has been scratched.

Those who missed *The Long Hot Summer* and have not yet been convinced that Don Johnson is an artist and a craftsman and not just today's heartthrob or another pretty face will change their minds when they see *Cease Fire*.

In that low-budget film, which he was shooting even as he waited to hear if his long shot as the star of the prospective series, *Miami Vice*, was going to pay off, Don lights up the screen.

He wears no Versace jackets, drives no Ferrari, has no cute pet. He plays a traumatized Vietnam veteran named Tim Murphy in the movie, and he's won plaudits for his electrifying portrayal of a man tormented by nightmares from his past and the Asian conflict that was a part of it. *Newsweek*'s Harry F. Waters praised Don for his performance, which "rings so searingly true that it could even inspire some moviegoers to reappraise their hurrahs for the comic-book heroics of Rambo."

It was a job that Don took—as he takes everything—very seriously. Even with his future as a television-series star hanging in the balance, he gave everything he had to the job at hand. The film premiered in Florida, where it was shot, and Don tearfully told a press conference of Vietnam vets that he was afraid he'd prove incapable of portraying the depth of their pain and anguish. He proved his capabilities to such a degree that the film might have established him even if the role of Sonny Crockett had gone to someone else.

But the role went to Don, of course, and any other conceivable future he might have had must be left to the imagination.

Instead of "who-knows-what?" we've got *Miami Vice,* the most talked-about, copied show on television. The series has already spawned imitations—*Hollywood Beat, The Insiders*—both of which are like cheap paste copies of the genuine diamond. It takes more than snappy editing, eccentric camera angles, and a flashy New Wave soundtrack to make magic.

Miami Vice as a show is as determined as Don Johnson as a star to keep getting better and better, to grow and stretch the boundaries of possibility. The *Vice* production team strives to be the newest, the hottest, the only game in town. Before the 1985 season began, producer John Nicolella announced confidently, "If anybody tries to imitate the show, they will be imitating *last* season's. . . . We're going to try to continue to top ourselves, to not repeat ourselves, to reach the limits."

They did this with the opening episode, by shooting the two-hour episode in Manhattan. With the confidence only one who's backed a winner can display, Nicolella said, "We're bringing New York to *Miami Vice,* not vice versa. This show has a hot, cosmopolitan look and style, and we are going to show that look and style as it exists in New York, instead of the gritty, hard-edged side of the city people usually see on television."

The episode truly did feature, as Nicolella had promised, shots of New York that are rarely seen, from Art Deco interiors to slick Soho lofts. And, as usual, it was the *Vice* team who called the shots, informing Jaynee Keyes, head of the Governor's Office of Motion Picture Development that they wanted no brick, no wood, no red, no earth tones. Miami Vice wasn't about to change *its* style, not for the Big Apple, at least. After all, apples don't fit into their color scheme.

Michael Mann set the scene, announcing *Miami Vice* planned to "do" New York the same way as Miami. That meant, for starters, no tourist attractions. No World Trade Center or Empire State Building or Forty-second Street. They wouldn't shoot New York as it usually was shot.

The cast and crew took Manhattan by storm, even drawing fifty journalists to a press conference held to announce that the press wouldn't be allowed on the set.

And so Crockett and Tubbs took a little business trip up north to New York City, Tubbs's home town (though he didn't seem to have anybody, even family, to look up while he was there), where they found little cooperation from the tough Manhattan detectives. The script, "Prodigal Son," used a finish that probably wouldn't have worked if the episode were dealing with any other city in the country: the bad guy at the top, the Mr. Big, was a blue-chip, blueblood tycoon. He saw drugs as just another financial commodity on the big board, like soybean futures or AT&T shares.

To open with a bang, *Vice* put together a dazzling cast that included the return of Pam Grier as Valerie and of Miguel Pinero. Pinero, as mesmerizing in the *Miami Vice* two-hour debut as Calderone, was now reincarnated as a Colombian dealer who, like Calderone, bumped off anyone who got in his way. Makeup and wardrobe made sure Pinero looked nothing like Calderone, the latter being such a powerful character he's sure to turn up again. As for Grier, the producer said, "When we find somebody who's so great, we keep them around. We might keep 'em locked up for 125 years, but we don't kill 'em off." And so Valerie, who only a year before had gone off to the big house for being too quick with a gun, was now out on the street, working as an informant and going a little too far with her cover for the crook sharing her bed. Of course, she shared that bed with Tubbs in the episode, too. And Don Johnson got the steamiest sex scene Sonny Crockett had ever had on the air. Since the boys are sex symbols, the *Vice* writers and producers are going for the sex.

In another nod to New York City, which *Vice*'s producer said had "design, style, and energy," a cameo was given to the Australian who's ended up more New Yorkish than most native New Yorkers, Peter Allen (John Nicolella, contrariwise, *is* a native New Yorker).

Just as it's redefining Miami, and New York, for Americans, *Miami Vice* is redefining the U.S.A. overseas, where it's been picked up as a regular series in several countries and where its two-hour opener was shown in theaters as a feature film in others.

Actually, *Miami Vice* has made its mark just about everywhere. Even cartoonist Gary Trudeau proved he's a viewer by using the series as the subject of a full week's worth of

"Doonesbury" cartoons. The most classic of these ended with the memorable line, "Sonny always wears mauve on a bust." Just goes to show what can happen when you send a two-pound box of chocolates to some guy's wife.

Other name guest stars signed up for *Miami Vice*'s 1985–86 season included Tina Turner, Julio Iglesias, Eartha Kitt, and Phil Collins, whose songs are so akin to the show's atmosphere. Collins was terrific playing a tacky game-show host in a fall episode. Another reprise on the second-time-around guest list was Glenn Frey, who appeared as a smuggler in the heralded episode based on his "Smuggler's Blues."

And it's not only the great guest stars that continue to set *Miami Vice* apart from and above its competition. It's all the great character parts, roles most actors would sign a pact with the devil to get a chance at. One of the most notable performances during 1985 was Bruce McGill's as a ex–vice cop who'd gone over the edge when the drug trafficker he'd fought for years to arrest was acquitted. It's those guest shots by stars and known actors (McGill was the beer-guzzling biker in *Animal House*) and unknowns that make *Miami Vice* the show around which viewers plan their Friday nights.

The series, should its ratings begin to droop, has an ace up its sleeve. It's screened on Friday evenings, a notoriously poor time to catch the younger audience. With a switch to midweek, the sky could be the limit. Not that it has to worry about competition on Fridays if it's on the same level as *Spenser: For Hire* and *Our Family Honor*. It seems almost self-destructive to schedule any other show dealing with cops and crooks opposite the series attorney and professor Alan Dershowitz (author of *The Best Defense*) termed the law-and-order show that "comes closest to conveying the complexities of the law."

If Don Johnson doesn't get bored with Sonny Crockett, it should take Americans a long, long time to get bored with Don. "I knew I could change my life," says the man who went from all-night partying to jogging, pumping iron (he doubled the time of his workouts to look his best for the bare-chested scenes in *The Long Hot Summer*), and eating lots of vegetables. Like Sonny Crockett, Don Johnson can best be summed up in one word: "survivor." He's had the drugs and the drinks and the dizzy girls Hollywood's so full of. Now he's more content with fishing, boating, and shooting a few rounds of golf. Survivors don't need exciting hobbies—they've already had exciting lives.

179

Life? Well, it's pretty much like Don Johnson says it is: "Sometimes you eat the bear, sometimes the bear eats you." This time he's eating the bear—and enjoying every single bite.

PAUL FERRIS

RICHARD BURTON

Actor. Every man's and every woman's idea of an
Actor, he strutted and brooded, all the world his stage.
Ever great in promise and mellifluous in delivery, he
up-staged and spellbound ordinary mortals. Rumpled
and rumbustious, he lived out his great part in public
places and in the public prints.

A man who was paid immense fortunes and spent
immense fortunes. A miner's son from the Welsh
Valleys who sported on the banks of Old Nile, great
Anthony to Elizabeth Taylor's Cleopatra, while the
world watched enthralled and only the money men
counted the cost.

Famous and unknown, ambiguously open, admired,
envied and despaired of. A man who adored women,
was oddly contemptuous of the actor's job and loved
words, the power of words, above all.

Full of sound and fury, a wide-screen spectacular. This
was his Life.

POST A LITTLE HAPPINESS

Post·A·Book

A Royal Mail service in association with the Book Marketing Council & The Booksellers Association.
Post-A-Book is a Post Office trademark.

LAUREN BACALL

BY MYSELF

'I loved Betty's book – don't miss it'
David Niven

In her own words, her own story – LAUREN BACALL
By Myself.

She writes the way she is, straightforward, funny,
honest, alive. At 19 the nice bright stage-struck New
York girl suddenly found herself in Hollywood – a
starring role, instant fame. And found Bogart, and
became his 'Baby' in one of the greatest of all
Hollywood romances – 'no one has ever written a
romance better than we lived it'.

After Bogart's tragic death, she fought back and
remade her life through the ups and downs of
emotional and professional involvements – becoming a
true star of Broadway and the movies. This marvellous
book is witness to her star qualities – as full of love,
laughter and honesty as Lauren Bacall herself.

'A marvellous book about a marvellous person'
Cosmopolitan

NEW ENGLISH LIBRARY

MARCIA CHELLIS

THE JOAN KENNEDY STORY

'I had no idea what I was getting into. I was just a nice young girl marrying a nice young man.'

A good Catholic girl, fresh out of a private college run by nuns, Joan Kennedy was marrying into the most glamorous and politically ambitious family in the US.

Within eighteen months, her brother-in-law was President. Two years later her husband Teddy was elected to the Senate and Joan was an ornamental presence at the glittering court of the new Camelot.

But behind the façade, her life was turning into a private hell. Faced not only by her new family's ruthless manipulation but with her husband's almost contemptuous infidelities, she had started on her tragedy-marked decline into alcoholism . . .

Her story is one of struggle and despair. Yet ultimately she triumphed with a final success in her escape both from alcoholism and from the clutches of the Kennedy family.

'Explosive'
Daily Express

'This is the book the Kennedy clan fears most'
Sunday Times

NEW ENGLISH LIBRARY

SENSATIONAL BIOGRAPHY AND AUTOBIOGRAPHY
FROM HODDER AND STOUGHTON PAPERBACKS

All these books are available at your local bookshop or newsagent, or can be ordered direct from the publisher. Just tick the titles you want and fill in the form below.

Prices and availability subject to change without notice.

Hodder & Stoughton Paperbacks, P.O. Box 11, Falmouth, Cornwall.

Please send cheque or postal order, and allow the following for postage and packing:

U.K. – 55p for one book, plus 22p for the second book, and 14p for each additional book ordered up to a £1.75 maximum.

B.F.P.O. and EIRE – 55p for the first book, plus 22p for the second book, and 14p per copy for the next 7 books, 8p per book thereafter.

OTHER OVERSEAS CUSTOMERS – £1.00 for the first book, plus 25p per copy for each additional book.

Name ....

Address..

....